RKO CLASSIC SCREENPLAYS

2/A

This Land is Mine

Directed by: Jean Renoir
Screenplay by: Dudley Nichols

An Andrew Velez Book

FREDERICK UNGAR PUBLISHING CO.
New York

Published by arrangement with RKO General, Inc.

PUBLISHER'S NOTE:
This is the complete final screenplay for the RKO film.
The movie as released may differ from the screenplay
in some respects.

Printed in Great Britain
by Biddles of Guildford

ISBN 0-8044-6698-X

INTRODUCTION

The year 1943 proved to be a very successful one for RKO. Profits at the box-office approached the $7 million mark. By today's standards that is not an impressive figure. When one considers, however, that the average ticket price for a movie then was a quarter or less, profits that reached hundreds of thousands of dollars, not to mention millions, become a much more significant achievement.

The war took a turn decisively in the Allies' favor during 1943. Films dealing with the war or some aspect of it were dominant among the important releases of the year. *Casablanca* won an Academy Award as the Best Picture of the Year. Among others were *Guadalcanal Diary, Bataan, Destination Tokyo, The Immortal Sergeant, So Proudly We Hail*, and *Stage Door Canteen*.

RKO released fifty films in 1943, only four of which did not earn a profit. Among its most successful offerings were *Tender Comrade, The Fallen Sparrow, Hitler's Children, Bombardier*, and *Behind the Rising Sun*. All of these were related to the war and reflected Hollywood's continuing and intense involvement.

Of the dozens of films RKO and other studios produced about World War II as it was seen as home and abroad, *This Land is Mine* was not the usual war melodrama. Directed by Jean Renoir and written by Dudley Nichols, it presented characters who showed both weaknesses and strengths instead of the usual array of good guys and bad guys.

At the beginning of the film the setting is identified as "somewhere in Europe," although clearly the location is meant to be Renoir's native France. At the same time there are touches throughout the picture such as a sign on a building wall reading "Buy Defense Bonds," which are distinctly American. Realism, in the naive sense, was not the purpose of the film. By interjecting elements that created a certain level of generalization, Renoir and Nichols made it possible for the audience to identify with the Nazi occupation of the town.

Renoir said, "This film . . . was made uniquely for America, to suggest to the Americans that daily life in an occupied country was not as simple as some people might assume . . . I thought of Daudet's *Contes du Lundi*, and it was while telling Daudet's story to Charles

Laughton that I had the idea . . . ". None of the melodramatic tributes to the Resistance (*Joan of Lorraine, 13 Rue Madeleine, The Seventh Cross*, etc.), explained any reasons for France's sudden collapse nor the complexity of the situation in which some decent Frenchmen felt they should support a collaborationist government.

Charles Laughton portrayed a cowardly, mother-dominated schoolteacher who is so fearful during an air raid that he becomes an object of derisive laughter to his students. The power of the film derives from the evolution he goes through as he becomes aware of the meaning of the Occupation and finds the strength within himself to resist it.

The film was a commercial success in the United States, although critic James Agee was moved to comment, "I find this sort of stodgy heroism, about such subjects, incredulously indecent." Critical disapproval was certainly nothing new for Renoir. *Rules of the Game*, now generally acknowledged to be his masterpiece, was one of his greatest commercial failures at its initial release in 1939. In 1962 it was chosen by an international poll of critics as the third greatest film ever made.

The films of his American experience were not among the director's favorites. Yet *Swamp Water* (1941), *The Southerner* (1945), etc., contain atmospheric and poetic elements characteristic of much of his work and remain worthy today of being seen with a fresh viewpoint.

Upon its release in France after the war, *This Land is Mine* was roundly attacked and subsequently withdrawn. A nation still suffering the effects of the war, wracked by political dissent, and eager to forget any less than glorious elements of its recent past was not interested in a film that sympathetically presented different points of view about the Occupation. Four decades later, France is still wrestling with the events of the war years and the actions of its citizens even as the impending trial of accused Nazi war criminal, Klaus Barbie, is likely to stir up further controversy and bitter feelings. Laboring under the disadvantage of not knowing personally what the Occupation was really like, Renoir nevertheless created a film in Hollywood unique and meaningful in its ideas of the realities of ordinary life during those traumatic years.

Andrew Velez

CAST:

Albert Lory	Charles Laughton
Louise Martin	Maureen O'Hara
George Lambert	George Sanders
Major Von Keller	Walter Slezak
Paul Martin	Kent Smith
Mrs. Emma Lory	Una O'Connor
Prof. Sorel	Philip Merivale
Mayor	Thurston Hall
Prosecuting Attorney	George Coulouris
Julie Grant	Nancy Gates
Presiding Judge	Ivan Simpson
Edmund Lorraine	John Donat
Lt. Schwartz	Frank Alten
Little Man	Leo Bulgakov
Mr. Lorraine	Wheaton Chambers
Mrs. Lorraine	Cecil Weston

CREDITS:

Screenplay	Dudley Nichols
Director	Jean Renoir
Production Designer	Eugene Lourié
Music	Lothar Perl
Musical Director	C. Bakaleinikoff
Director of Photography	Frank Redman, A.S.C.
Art Directors	Albert S. D'Agostino
	Walter E. Keller
Special Effects	Vernon L. Walker, A.S.C.
Dialogue Director	Leo Bulgakov
Set Decorations	Darrell Silvera
	Al Fields
Recorded by	John E. Tribby
Rerecorded by	James G. Stewart
Gowns	Renié
Edited by	Frederic Knudtson
Assistant Director	Edward Donahoe

NOTE

The locale is symbolic of all Occupied countries and hence resembles no one precisely. Neither sets nor manners should be too foreign. We make a complete translation of an alien people. They speak plain English and we avoid any accents except in the Germans. They speak as you do, they have about the same habits as you have, they could be yourselves. Everything is translated into English, even the signs in the street and the headlines in the newspapers.

Albert Lory (CHARLES LAUGHTON) . . . a schoolmaster who is on the sunny side of fifty and secretly loves:

Louise Martin (MAUREEN O'HARA) . . . also a teacher, about twenty-five years old. She is in love with:

George Lambert (George Sanders) . . . who works at the railroad terminal in the town. A well-built, good-looking man in his thirties.

Major Erich von Keller (Walter Slezak) . . . the German commander in the occupied town. Very well educated, gallant, amusing and with an astute mind.

Mrs. Emma Lory (Una O'Connor) . . . mother of Albert. Nearing seventy. Don't be fooled by her walking with a cane, she's a very strong woman. Loves Albert possessively and inordinately, but is a domestic tyrant.

Paul Martin (Kent Smith) . . . Louise's brother and a couple of years older than she is. He works in the switch tower at the railroad terminal.

Professor Sorel (Philip Merivale) . . . a grand old man of seventy, principal of the school. A scholar and an independent character.

Mayor Henry Manville (Thurston Hall) . . . also seventy. The most important man in town and he knows it.

Julie Grant (Nancy Gates) . . . the fiancee of Paul Martin. A sweet, charming girl in her early twenties. A good friend of Louise.

Lieutenant Schwartz . . . adjutant to Major von Keller. As severe as the major is friendly. He is the ears and eyes of Von Keller and is a perfect soldier.

Edmond Lorraine (John Donat) . . . a delicate boy of ten, Albert's favorite pupil.

Mr. Lorraine . . . father of Edmond.

Mrs. Lorraine . . . mother of Edmond.

Presiding Judge . . .

Second Judge . . .

Prosecutor (Ian Wolfe) . . .

AND OTHERS.

NOTES ON SCORE

This script is designed for an arranged score rather than a new composition. We prefer to use certain themes and movements from great music of the past, for we are dealing with an old civilization and wish to illustrate it musically. We are not afraid of using known music; in fact if the audience recognizes the music it is all to the good. We desire the associations which the music will evoke.

For instance, over the titles and during the first part of the prologue, which symbolizes the death of a town through war and defeat, and the impending doom of the Nazis marching on the town, we would use probably the first movement from Beethoven's Fifth Symphony, which is a kind of "knocking at the door of fate." This movement would continue until we actually see the German troops entering the town — and then there would be no music but only the ominous sound of the troops, the clanking of tanks, grinding of military lorries, the tread of marching feet and so on. These grim sounds are heard over the series of scenes of people watching from behind closed shutters, people praying in the church, and all the glimpses of personal reactions to the occupation of the town by the enemy.

But the moment the mayor and the German commander shake hands — over the closeup of their hands which symbolizes collaboration — we begin to hear Wagner's "The Valkyrie," which is a triumphant over-riding of power and might, and this continues over all the swift images of bursting activity in the town, at the railroad, in the factories and everywhere else, activity which is to feed the German war machine.

But a new note is struck when we come to the secret and illegal printing press where resistance is being preached. Here we have a theme for "liberty" — an old 18th century French melody "Le Chant du Depart," by Mehul. This was the song of Valmy, of all the big victories over the Germans during the time of the French Revolution in 1792, and it is in its feeling almost a musical representation of our own American liberators — Jefferson, Washington et cetera. This theme will be heard softly over the secrecy of the printing press and we hear a few bars of it whenever we see the illegal paper "Liberty."

And later on in the film when the theme of freedom emerges through the actions of Albert Lory we hear the refrain again. We will hear it faintly when he reads the Declaration of the Rights of Man and as he is taken out to be executed it becomes choral music, swelling up triumphantly at the very end.

We shall find an old love song for the accordion which Paul plays and which Albert hears in his prison cell — the theme which represents the love of Albert for Louise. Over the flower picking scene with Edmond, which should have a sort of tender fairyland quality, we shall use something delicate and charming, perhaps the minuet from Mozart's "Don Juan."

FOREWORD

Somewhere in Europe. This Town is half the World today: we fight to keep it from being all the World tomorrow.

THIS LAND IS MINE

FADE IN

EXTERIOR SKY—DAY
Close angle up on a limp flag being pulled down a flagpole against a somber sky. We cannot see the nationality of the flag.

EXTERIOR FRENCH STREET—DAY
Long shot—Town Hall and we see where the flag is as it is pulled down; atop the Town Hall at end of street. Street empty, no life visible.

EXTERIOR FRENCH STREET—ANOTHER SECTION—DAY
Shot down—another section of French street, showing all shutters closed, no life visible. Near camera a stripped auto, its bones picked of everything removable, lies against the curb.

EXTERIOR NEW YORK STREET—DAY
Shot down—empty street. All shutters closed. No life. A few pigeons feeding in middle of street near camera, nothing else beyond.

EXTERIOR CIMARRON STREET—DAY
Long shot—section of street, camera in front of railroad warehouse at end. An abandoned streetcar halfway down street, its trolly pole off the wire. Near camera a lost dog wanders around, or digs a bone from the dust. No other life.

EXTERIOR RAILROAD YARD—DAY—(LOCATION)
Full shot—many tracks and immobile trains and freight cars. Nothing moving, no sign of life.

INTERIOR RAILROAD SWITCH TOWER—DAY—(Set on stage)
Empty and lifeless. Spider webs and dust on the levers that work the switches. An old coat, abandoned, hung on one lever. A couple of pigeons are sitting on the sill of the open window. Another pigeon flies out through window from behind camera.

EXTERIOR FREIGHT OFFICE—DAY—(End of Cimarron Street)
Camera first on roof on which is lettered "Freight Office" and then pan down to the little yard outside enclosed by a fence with a gateway to street in it. An abandoned dray or wagon, without horses, stands in this small yard, several packing cases which have been open and the contents taken out by marauders on the wagon. A flock of pigeons feeding in the yard around the wagon.

INTERIOR FREIGHT OFFICE—DAY—(On stage)
No freight, no movement, no life. Floor littered with old newspapers. A gust of wind blows more newspaper in through the open door and also blows old bills of lading from the desk to the floor. (This is later on George Lambert's desk) Through window behind desk we see the switch tower against the sky. A cat prowls around in search of mice.

EXTERIOR LOADING CORRAL—DAY—(LOCATION)

Shooting across the empty straw-littered pens we see an empty cattle car on the tracks at further edge. No cattle, no life. Door of cattle car yawns open.

INTERIOR FACTORY—DAY—(STOCK)
A vista of idle machinery. Nothing turning or moving. No men. (Vern Walker effect)

INTERIOR FACTORY OFFICE—DAY
Shooting across a dusty desk where a mouse nibbles a stale crust of bread we see the idle machinery through an open door that swings in the wind. Perhaps also see machinery through windows. On other desk are dusty typewriters, paper still in them.

EXTERIOR CIMARRON STREET—DAY
Close shot—poster on fence which encloses the small freight yard. It shows a tank, with Allied flags spread above it, and above this is lettered: "WE WILL WIN BECAUSE WE ARE THE STRONGEST." (Not a new poster) Over this we hear a clanking and growing noise and camera pans to take in a tank coming up street past the abandoned street car. As it comes near we see the German swastika painted on it. Swastika comes right into and past camera. Then we see German soldiers coming on motorcycles, machine guns ready. Then an armored car, then trucks full of German soldiers, machine guns ready. Swastikas on all the cars.

EXTERIOR NEW YORK STREET—DAY
Shot down street as noise of Germans is heard. Street empty, shutters closed. A baby playing at curb. A door is flung open near camera, a woman dashes out, seizes baby, runs in and slams door behind her, just as the Germans appear around corner and come marching up street: (Same troops, motorcycles, trucks, etc.) As they pass camera—

EXTERIOR FRENCH STREET—DAY

3

The German troops come around a bend or corner and come moving toward camera, filling the street, the noise of their motorcycles and trucks growing louder and more ominous. As they pass camera—

EXTERIOR STREET—IN FRONT OF CHURCH—DAY
Germans passing in full shot, paying no attention to the church.

EXTERIOR CASTLE IN NOTRE DAME STREET—DAY
German troops moving past. Noise. A sense of overwhelming power in these cuts and movements, of all sections of a large town filling up with the conquerors.

EXTERIOR NEW YORK STREET—DAY
Close moving shot on faces of half a dozen German soldiers in a truck watching windows of street. We see backs of half a dozen others watching opposite walls. Soldiers' faces are expressionless, machine-like, suggesting brute power, devoid of any individual thinking. They look up at—
Reverse angle—moving along on shuttered windows.
Closed shutters in street. Above shutters we read:
                    Department Store
We hear trucks and troops. Camera moves up close.

INTERIOR STORE—DAY
Close shot on faces of Mr. Lorraine, his wife, and their ten-year-old son, Edmond, a slight sensitive boy. They peek fearfully through chinks in shutters giving streaked light on their faces. Their expression full of silent despair. (We hear troops in street.)

INTERIOR BEHIND ANOTHER PAIR OF SHUTTERS—
DAY
We see a family peering through chinks which light their faces. Despairing, broken faces. A little girl tugs at her mother's dress, "Mama, let me see." The mother whispers "Sssssh."

INTERIOR BEHIND SHUTTERS—DAY

4

Close shot—George Lambert looking through chinks into street where we hear the passing Germans. His face is without expression; we don't know what he is thinking.

INTERIOR PROFESSOR SOREL'S OFFICE IN SCHOOL— DAY
Very close shot of the old man, Sorel, feeding his two canaries in a small cage that hangs beside a shuttered window. We hear the Germans passing but Sorel refuses to look out, for it is too painful to him.

INTERIOR CHURCH—DAY
Medium shot—small group knelt down before a small shrine in an alcove. Two men and three women, with an old priest knelt down in their midst. (One of the men is one of the printers we shall see later.) Their prayer is silent but from the street outside we hear the passing Germans.

INTERIOR BEHIND ANOTHER PAIR OF UPSTAIRS SHUTTERS—DAY
An old man and a very old woman, poor people, peering through chinks. She has a shawl about her. The old man, almost trembling, mutters "Swine." His wife puts her arm around his shoulders fearfully: "Shhhh." She crosses herself.

EXTERIOR STREET—DAY
Camera moves from a shuttered ground-floor window to the only open window in the street. Stops on:

EXTERIOR WINDOW IN STREET—DAY
Close shot of three people watching the troops enter the town. This is the house of Louise and Paul Martin. Paul, smoking a cigarette, has his arm around a pretty young girl, Julie Grant. His expression contrasts with his sister's. Louise watches with silent hatred; she doesn't accept this defeat. Julie is very angry and shows it. Paul is ironical and almost indifferent. A German voice calls out from behind camera.

5

GERMAN VOICE: You—you there in the window!

EXTERIOR STREET—DAY
Reverse angle on soldiers in truck. One of them raising a machine gun as a corporal calls in bad English:
CORPORAL: Shut that window!

EXTERIOR WINDOW—DAY
Close shot on three. Paul smiles and waves. Julie makes a face at the Germans.
PAUL: Okay. Take it easy, pal.
Starts closing shutters.

EXTERIOR STREET—DAY
Reverse on soldiers in trucks. The soldier lowers his gun as truck moves on slowly up street. He watches:
Shutters closing from soldier's angle—camera moving slowly to bring us to shuttered window of next house.

INTERIOR LORY HOME—DAY
Behind shuttered window (of house which adjoins Martin's). Close shot—Albert Lory and his mother, Mrs. Emma Lory. He is crying, as his mother tries to comfort him. She is indignant with the Germans for making her son cry.
MRS. LORY: Albert! Your handkerchief!
ALBERT: Yes, Mother.
He gets it out fumblingly and clumsily and wipes his face, looking like a ridiculous little boy for all his years and plumpness.

EXTERIOR TOWN HALL—DAY
Shooting past statue we see the Germans now filling the street, coming toward camera. The statue represents a dying soldier and on it in foreground is a plaque which reads in part:
"1914-1918
In memory of those who
died to bring Peace to
the World."

Camera pulls back to longer angle and we see more Germans filling the street. Soldiers jump down from the trucks and form a guard in front of the Town Hall as a Mercedes car comes swiftly toward camera, passing trucks and soldiers. The men salute as the car passes. Car stops in front of Town Hall. Guard salutes. A German captain, in charge of the guard, steps forward and salutes Major von Keller who climbs from the car with his adjutant, Lieutenant Schwartz. Schwartz's eyes are taking in everything very swiftly; he sees everything.

CAPTAIN: *(in German to Von Keller)* The mayor is waiting for you, sir.

VON KELLER: *(in German)* Good. His name is Manville, isn't it?

Close shot—group as the sergeant replies in the affirmative. Von Keller extends his right arm and now we see that his left arm is rigid and useless at his side, it always hangs stiffly down, a white glove over a stiff, lifeless hand. Schwartz slips a white glove onto Von Keller's extended right hand and they turn to enter the Town Hall, an ironical look of amusement on the German major's face. Camera pans on them as they enter the Town Hall and then camera moves toward a window to look in. As camera pans past a poster, we

WIPE

INTERIOR CITY HALL—DAY

Shot through window of city hall. Through window we see Mayor Manville drawn up with his council to receive Von Keller. Manville is a man of sixty, very important and authoritative, with a white moustache, dark suit and wing collar. With him are the chief of police (no uniform) and a couple of secretaries. We see but don't hear a short colloquy. Von Keller is punctilious and we see the mayor bowing and eager to please. Finally they shake hands. Insert the handshake. Von Keller's aristocratic white-gloved hand takes the strong bare hand of Manville.

Angle up on flagpole as the Swastika is run up and flutters briskly in the wind in contrast with the limp flag we saw pulled down.

EXTERIOR RAILROAD YARD—DAY
Everything moving, trains hooting, backing, switching, loaded cars.

INTERIOR RAILROAD SWITCH TOWER—DAY
Very busy, switches being pulled as trains are shunted around. (Paul Martin operating switches.)

INTERIOR FREIGHT OFFICE—DAY
Shooting past George Lambert, who is motioning some men with handtrucks, we see a very busy scene—everything moving.

INTERIOR FULL WAREHOUSE—DAY
Through open doors we see busy trains. Men moving goods out of warehouse. As boxes and crates are wheeled swiftly past camera, we see their various destinations: Duesseldorf, Hamburg, Berlin, Nuremburg, Bremen, etc.

INTERIOR FACTORY—DAY
Everything turning and now we add to the medley of sounds the whirring of wheels, grinding, clacking, hissing steam, flapping of belts, whistles, hammers, etc.

INTERIOR FACTORY OFFICE—DAY
The dust and mice are gone. Clerks working, typewriters going, men entering and exiting with bills of lading. Through doors and windows we see the spinning, whirring machines. Production, production, production!

EXTERIOR STOCKYARD NEAR RAILROAD—DAY (LOCATION L.A.)
Shooting through gate we see lowing cattle being herded past on their way to loading corral.
(Try to pick up shots into stockyard pens showing milling sheep and cattle.)

EXTERIOR LOADING CORRAL—DAY (LOCATION L.A.)

Shooting across pens filled with cattle, we see a cattle car on tracks at far gate. Men busily driving the cattle into the car. As the last cattle are herded in camera zooms to open door just as it is being slid shut. The destination "Berlin" is lettered on the door and it slides into frame as door slides shut and is locked by the loaders.

EXTERIOR FRENCH STREET—DAY
Full shot—down street. Few German soldiers patrolling the street, but the populace is gathered in queues before certain shops.

EXTERIOR BUTCHER SHOP—DAY
Full shot—queue, mostly tired women and old people in line waiting for the butcher. Camera moves in along faces of women, women, women, resigned anxious faces with empty market bags. As we reach the butcher's counter we find people from our story in this order (though we don't yet know them as characters). First an unknown woman, giving the butcher her ration book coupon. Second Mrs. Lory, third Mrs. Lorraine, fourth the little girl Emilie from Louise's class. The others are nondescript. The butcher takes a tiny piece of meat, takes the first woman's coupon for it, then tells the others:
BUTCHER: Sorry. No more meat.
MRS. LORY: *(looks at him indignantly)* Why not tell us two hours ago? I've been standing here since seven o'clock!

DISSOLVE

INTERIOR DARK CELLAR—NIGHT
We see figures of three men silhouetted against a dim light over a small printing press which is running.
Camera moves in as one of the men picks a paper from the press and we see it as a small illegal newspaper with the caption LIBERTY across the top. (Show faces of men in light reflected from paper so we will remember them.)

DISSOLVE

9

Insert in darkness as a hand mysteriously slips one of the papers under a street door.
Insert hand pushing a paper through shutters of a window.
Insert hand dropping a paper through mail slot in a door.
Insert hand sliding a paper under a door.

DISSOLVE

INTERIOR LORY HOUSE—DAY
Close shot down on the paper which has been slid under the rug, but we can still see part of the word liberty.
Pan up and we are in the downstairs room of the Lory home. It is early in the morning and we see Mrs. Lory come in from the kitchen and set the breakfast table. She has something which is obviously very important—a wine bottle which contains about a half-pint of milk. (The high chair Albert used as a child stands in a corner of room. Pictures on wall of Albert as a child and of her dead husband, a man of about thirty.)
Close shot—Mrs. Lory as she proudly puts the bottle in the center of the table and fixes a newspaper around it to conceal it for a surprise. It is an official newspaper and we note the headline: HITLER SPEAKS FOR UNITED EUROPE. Then, having fixed it to her satisfaction, she goes to bottom of stairway and calls up.
MRS. LORY: Albert?

INTERIOR ALBERT'S BEDROOM UPSTAIRS—DAY
Close shot—Albert half-dressed, washing his face at the wash-stand. He raises a dripping face and calls back to stairway. (A collection of butterflies, behind glass, hangs on the wall.)
ALBERT: Yes, Mother.
MRS. LORY'S VOICE: Hurry up, darling. Don't forget to brush your teeth.
ALBERT: No, Mother.
He dries his face as we hear a miaow and he brightens up as he turns to look past camera at:

10

Close shot—front dormer window. A friendly cat which is on the tiles or in the rain gutter outside is asking to be let in. (The cat has a bell attached to its collar.) Camera pulls back a little as Albert enters, opens window and lets it in with many endearments. He is stroking and fondling the cat, which seems to mean something to him which we don't yet understand, when he sees Edmond Lorraine, the small boy who lives above the department store across the street, opening the shutters of the upstairs window across the narrow street. The boy calls out.

EDMOND: Good morning, Mr. Lory.

ALBERT: *(his face lights up)* Oh, good morning, Edmond. *(shakes finger at him)* Don't forget to brush your teeth.

EDMOND: No, sir, I won't.

As Edmond vanishes, his father, a middle-aged merchant, appears in the window. Leans out and speaks about his son, with a kind of wink, knowing his son is a good pupil.

MR. LORRAINE: How is—(indicates back of him)—the boy getting along at school?

ALBERT: *(a little shy and self-conscious as he was not with the boy)* Oh—very well. Very well, Mr. Lorraine. I—

Breaks off and looks down, as does Lorraine across the street.

EXTERIOR STREET—DAY
Shot down past him through window. We see a German patrol walking past in street.

INTERIOR ALBERT'S BEDROOM—DAY
Shot from behind Albert as he quickly closes the window and we see Mr. Lorraine do the same thing simultaneously. His mother's voice calls sharply up the stairs again and makes him almost jump.

MRS. LORY'S VOICE: Albert!

ALBERT: Yes, Mother.

MRS. LORY'S VOICE: Hurry up, darling. You'll be late.

As he puts the cat on the bed and hurriedly finishes his dressing—

INTERIOR LORY HOUSE—DOWNSTAIRS ROOM—DAY

Mrs. Lory comes in and sets a steaming cup of coffee on the table, looks to see everything is there for her son, whose footsteps we hear overhead. Then she goes over to clock and sets it five minutes fast, from 7:25 to 7:30. As the hand reaches the half hour it bongs and immediately she closes the clock, picks up a cane and raps the ceiling.

MRS. LORY: Darling!

ALBERT'S VOICE: *(very obedient)* Yes, Mother. Coming.

We hear him clump down the stairs and immediately the mother leans a little on her stick, as if setting the stage for her own entrance rather than her son's. He enters happily with the cat under his arm and kisses his mother. Mrs. Lory observes the cat and we see she doesn't like it, but she says nothing.

ALBERT: *(continued)* Good morning, Mother. How is your rheumatism?

MRS. LORY: Oh, I hardly slept a wink. I'm sure it's going to rain. It never fails.

Whereas she was quite active when alone, she now limps a little toward the table, using her stick and provoking sympathy. Albert, as soon as her back is turned, sets the clock back five minutes to the right time.

MRS. LORY: *(continued) (at table, with a little concealed excitement)* Now come sit down, darling. Don't let your breakfast get cold.

As he comes to the table—

MRS. LORY: *(continued)* Here's the newspaper.

ALBERT: *(looks at propped paper with disgust)* Newspaper! Lies!

MRS. LORY: *(with a quick warning glance at street windows)* Sssh! *(drops voice and indicates paper as he sits down)* You may find something interesting in it today.

He picks up the paper and reveals the bottle of milk. She smiles delightedly as he reacts with astonishment, and we see milk is precious and scarce.

ALBERT: Milk!

MRS. LORY: *(all smiles, very proud)* A whole half pint!

ALBERT: *(looks at her with round eyes)* How did you get it?

12

MRS. LORY: *(proud of her cleverness)* The doctor gave me a prescription.
ALBERT: *(with quick anxiety, naively)* Are you sick, Mother?
MRS. LORY: *(instantly playing for sympathy)* Have I ever been well? Never since you were born. Not that I blame you, my darling.
Anxiously he pours it into a glass and offers it to her but she rejects it with a grimace.
MRS. LORY: *(continued)* Not for me. You know I can't stand milk. Never could.
He looks a little baffled.
MRS. LORY: *(continued)* There's no reason why you shouldn't take advantage of my condition. You were so weak as a child. The only way I saved your life was by giving you plenty of milk. It's shocking now—so many cows in the country and no milk. *(sees some hairs on his coat sleeve)* Look at your coat. That filthy cat! Here, take it off. Let me brush it. *(takes off his coat as if he were still a little boy)* I wish that girl would keep her cat at home where it belongs. That's why I couldn't sleep—that yowling all night on the roof.
ALBERT: *(in a small voice)* I thought it was your rheumatism, Mother.
MRS. LORY: My rheumatism *and* the cat. You drink your milk.
She limps more noticeably as she exits with his coat to brush it. Albert looks after her uneasily and as she goes out we hear the cat make a plaintive miaow. Albert in the act of drinking the milk looks down at—
Closeup—cat on floor looking up at him and making a silent begging miaow.
Close shot—Albert taking in cat on floor. Very furtively he pours milk into a saucer and puts it under the table for the cat which begins lapping it greedily. Now we hear the mother's voice from the adjoining room as he drinks his coffee and eats his breakfast, keeping an anxious eye on the cat.
MRS. LORY'S VOICE: Some people are getting milk—and they don't need a prescription for it either. I hear at the Mayor's house they have cream on the table, every morning, a whole pitcher of it. Oh, he's doing all right, our Mayor. And so are the merchants. Black markets—that's why they have no food to sell on the coupons—selling

13

meat and butter out the back door for ten times its price. But nobody thinks of raising your salary, my dear. The schoolmaster must starve while men who can't even spell their own names get rich. *Her voice gets louder and she returns. Albert furtively conceals the cat, which is under table, with his legs. Guiltily he drops the newspaper and picks up the empty saucer under it and sets it on table.*

MRS. LORY: *(continued)* But at least we have order. Things are quiet now in the town, thank the Lord, and I suppose we shouldn't complain. We keep our place and *they* keep theirs. *(holds his jacket to put it on and sees milk left in his glass)* Finish your milk, you bad boy. *Shot from doorway as he drains the glass and she helps him on with his coat. Something under camera catches her eye.*

MRS. LORY: What's that?

She comes to camera and picks up the illegal paper that was half pushed under the rug. Albert comes to her and both look at it in close shot. Startled reactions.

MRS. LORY: *(continued) (whispers uneasily)* "Liberty."

Albert takes it from her and reads in a low halting voice as her face tightens with anxiety.

ALBERT: "Citizens, do not believe in the generosity of the conquerors. If they are not driven out of our land it means generations of slavery for our people. We must resist. Let each of us say to himself, 'This land is mine' . . ."

MRS. LORY: *(interrupts in a sharp whisper)* Trouble makers!

ALBERT: *(in timid agreement)* It's dangerous, Mother. I'd better burn it.

She nods and he starts for the stove in the room but she stops him with a sharp whisper, keeping an eye on the street windows.

MRS. LORY: Not here. They might see you. *(points upstairs to his room and then indicates windows)* I'll watch here. You can't even trust your neighbors nowadays.

He nods guiltily and starts swiftly up the stairs. Mrs. Lory moves close to the street window and watches out through the curtain. Shot past her at window. We see two civilians, workmen, pass along in the street.

14

INTERIOR ALBERT'S BEDROOM—DAY
Close shot—low camera—on Albert stooped before a small fireplace in which there are scraps of paper which he is lighting with a match. As the papers flare up he takes the small illegal newspaper from his jacket and starts to hold it in the blaze. The flame curls brightly behind the word "Liberty." Something comes into his face and we see an inner struggle. He just can't bring himself to burn that word "Liberty" and he glances around furtively to make sure his mother has not come up, then with his hands extinguishes the burning corner of paper, folds it quickly, gets up, looks around for a hiding place.

Another angle as Albert goes to the framed butterfly collection of his childhood, pulls it from the wall a little and secretes the newspaper behind it. He takes a look to see it is safely hidden, then hurries downstairs.

INTERIOR LORY HOUSE—DOWNSTAIRS ROOM
Albert's mother is watching at window. She sees out of the corner of her eye the cat jump up on the table and she runs at it and frightens it off as Albert comes down. The cat runs to Albert and he picks it up as he goes to the door.

MRS. LORY: *(impatiently)* That cat!

He collects some pupils' copybooks and puts them in a briefcase as she gets his hat for him.

MRS. LORY: *(continued)* Hurry, you'll be late for school.

ALBERT: *(kisses her obediently)* Good-bye, Mother.

She brushes a speck off his collar and fixes his tie, very possessively and fondly, and opens the door for him and he goes out with the cat in his arms. She closes the door but keeps a crack open through which she can watch him as he goes along the sidewalk to the next house.

EXTERIOR STREET—FRONT OF THE MARTINS' HOUSE
NEXT DOOR—DAY

15

Paul Martin is finishing pumping up a leaky tire of his bicycle at the curb as Albert comes along sidewalk and greets him. (Door of house in background.)

ALBERT: Good morning, Paul.

PAUL: *(looks up)* Oh, hello, Mr. Lory.

ALBERT: Where is Louise?

Before Paul can answer the door opens and Louise Martin with her hat on, her purse and some schoolbooks under her arm, comes out, taking the key from her purse to lock the door. She smiles at Albert as he lifts his hat and takes the cat to her shyly.

LOUISE: So there's the runaway. Has she been annoying your mother again?

ALBERT: *(embarrassedly)* Oh, not at all. We're very fond of her.

EXTERIOR LORY HOUSE—DAY
Close shot—Mrs. Lory's face as seen through a crack in the door of the next house. Her expression is eloquent and we see she doesn't like Louise any more than the cat.

EXTERIOR STREET—DAY
Medium shot—Albert, Louise and Paul who has finished pumping the tire and is putting the small pump in the tool case strapped to the bicycle. Louise takes the cat from Albert, puts it inside, closes and locks the door and puts the key in her purse as they join the waiting brother. Albert, self-conscious in the presence of Louise, tries to make conversation but only succeeds in muttering inaudibly.

ALBERT: Lovely weather.

LOUISE: What?

ALBERT: *(drops his briefcase and then speaks louder, with an effort, as he picks it up)* Lovely weather.

LOUISE: Oh, yes. Lovely.

Camera moves on them as they walk toward the school. Albert would like to talk to her but we see it is too difficult. Louise is very nice to him. Paul, with a friendly glance at Albert, addresses Louise—

PAUL: Why don't you ask him for dinner? *(smiles at Albert)* We're going to have a real feast tonight.

LOUISE: *(to Albert)* Yes, why don't you? George Lambert's coming.

PAUL: *(teasing)* Coming? He's bringing the dinner! *(grins to Albert)* She's got George chasing *pigeons*.

LOUISE: Paul, don't be silly!

PAUL: What's silly about anything to eat? *(grins to Albert, teasing Louise)* I couldn't figure out yesterday what George was doing up on the roof of the freight office. I found out last night when he brought my sister a mess of pigeons . . . He's got traps up there. *(laughs)*

LOUISE: *(trying to shut up the tease)* Will you come, Mr. Lory?

ALBERT: *(embarrassed)* Oh, thank you—but my mother—doesn't like to be left alone. You know she's—not very well.

LOUISE: Oh, I'm sorry—

Then she speaks swiftly, with alarm, seeing what we do: Paul pull one of the illegal papers carelessly from his inside pocket.

LOUISE: *(continued)* Paul!

Paul just grins at her and holds the paper toward Albert who flinches away from it as they all stop short.

PAUL: If you have to stay home and read you might as well have something interesting.

LOUISE: *(with sharp warning, startled; Albert backs from the paper)* Paul! Don't be crazy! *Watch out!*

PAUL: *(carelessly)* Why?

LOUISE: *(under her breath, frightened as she sees someone coming out of scene)* Soldiers!

Albert pales as they look across street at:
Two German soldiers coming toward camera on patrol along the opposite sidewalk. As they come close we can see our three in medium long shot and Paul calls to them.

PAUL: Hey, Kurt! Want to read something?

The soldiers start across toward the three.
Medium three shot at other side. Louise freezes and Albert grows pale, rooted to the spot, as Paul steps ahead in a friendly fashion and the two soldiers enter to him.

17

PAUL: Looks like someone's trying to compete with our official newspaper.

Kurt, the first soldier, takes the paper quickly and with a humorless face.

SOLDIER: Where you get this, Paul?

PAUL: *(shrugs)* Under the door.

Close shot—Louise and Albert. She is looking indignantly at her brother while Albert is just plain scared.

Group shot. The first soldier hands the paper to his companion and his expression is grim.

SOLDIER: We find many of these already. All over town.

PAUL: *(frowns)* Yeah?

SOLDIER: If you find any more, you tell us, Paul.

PAUL: Sure.

Before passing on the soldiers look at Albert searchingly.

SOLDIER: Any at your house?

Albert shakes his head, too frightened to speak and the soldiers pass on, talking in German between themselves. Louise comes over to her brother, followed by Albert. She is very angry but very quiet.

LOUISE: *(in a low voice)* You're very smart, aren't you?

PAUL: *(lightly)* Listen, I don't want to get in any trouble. They're all right, Louise. They're only doing their job.

LOUISE: *(quietly scathing)* And are you doing yours?

PAUL: *(throws his leg over bike, making fun of her seriousness)* Sure, just as fast as I can get there. *(grins)* Why jump on me? You don't say anything to George.

He pedals off out of scene, giving her no further chance to vent her indignation. Louise stands beside Albert, watching with a worried frown.

LOUISE: I don't understand my brother.

ALBERT: *(nervously)* Do you think they'll search the other houses?

JULIE'S VOICE: *(calls out of scene)* Hi, Paul!

Angle past them. Down the street we see Paul pull into the curb and stop his bicycle as a girl, Julie, runs out of the door of a house. She turns and waves to Louise who waves back.

18

EXTERIOR FRONT OF JULIE'S HOUSE—DAY
Medium shot—Paul and Julie as he gets her on the bar of his bike so he can carry her with him. She is laughing, as gay and pert as a monkey.
JULIE: Don't tear my stockings!
PAUL: *(laughs teasingly as he shoves off, balancing her)* You're just like all women—Thinking of your legs all the time.

EXTERIOR STREET—DAY
Medium close shot—Louise and Albert watching them. But Louise is hardly seeing them, worrying about her brother's behaviour, and Albert doesn't see them at all, worrying about that paper he hid in his bedroom.
Camera trucks ahead of them as they walk on toward school.
LOUISE: *(looking straight ahead)* It worries me—the way he's making friends with these—*(her tone is full of contempt)* —these soldiers.
ALBERT: *(looking straight ahead, anxiously—not making any sense)* I'll just say I didn't know anything about it.
LOUISE: *(not hearing, looking straight ahead, very worried)* He never was afraid of anything—and I know he's honest.

INTERIOR OFFICE OF PROFESSOR SOREL IN SCHOOL—DAY
Full shot. Professor Sorel, a fine-looking man of seventy, with a look of elegance about him in spite of his baggy, loose-fitting clothes, is feeding his canaries in a cage that hangs beside the window which overlooks the schoolyard, while Mayor Manville is very busy behind him, taking schoolbooks from shelves along the wall and piling them on a table, checking from a list which he has in his hand. (A large print, a primitive Pieta, on wall over fireplace.)
Close shot—Sorel as he turns from the birds and looks out the window, his hands in his baggy pockets, staring out thoughtfully. His manner disapproves what the Mayor is doing but he is holding his tongue. Through the window past him we see children

19

straggling across the courtyard toward the school, carrying satchels, some of them romping and playing, others walking more slowly. Sorel absently changes his glasses (it is a habit he has) removing his reading glasses, taking another pair from his handkerchief pocket and putting them on so he can watch the children. Albert and Louise enter the yard gate and come toward school. Close shot—Mayor at table with Sorel in background, his back to us. The mayor has finished his list and now he pushes the books into a stack as he turns to Sorel.

MAYOR: These must be burned, Professor Sorel.

Close shot—Sorel as he turns around into camera, quietly.

SOREL: By your order, Mr. Mayor, or by order of the enemy?

Two shot—as the mayor looks pained, raising a hand of protest.

MAYOR: Not by my order, my dear Sorel. Look, I'm here because I'm your friend. We've known each other all our lives. Perhaps we held different ideas, but I respect you. It's not my job, and not my wish, to do this—*(indicates books)*—but it is my job as Mayor to remove friction. *(confidentially)* It's our duty to preserve the life of this town, and the only way is to collaborate with the occupying authorities.

SOREL: *(indicates condemned books)* By burning truth?

MAYOR: *(very friendly)* My dear old friend, what does it matter in a time of crisis—a little more or less truth? Perhaps the untruth was in our past. We've always taught in our schools that the important history of our country began with the revolution. We were obsessed with individual freedom and the Rights of Man. We forgot the necessity of Authority and obedience—and so lost discipline. Without discipline we had strikes and political disorders. People did not agree. Look how our young people behaved—flouting their parents, thinking only of pleasure, parties, girls. Young men wanted cars. In our time we had no cars, my dear Sorel.

SOREL: *(dryly)* Maybe the reason was that there *were* no cars.

MAYOR: *(stiffening)* You must agree that we need discipline.

SOREL: *(quietly)* You mean by discipline that we should become servants of the enemy and help them to conquer other free peoples?

MAYOR: *(righteously)* You're not showing much understanding of the nature of this national ordeal. Perhaps God ordained it to teach us

20

how to live. We suffer, yes—but maybe it is for our own good. We must get back to family, duty, hard work, obedience—*(with a touch of coldness)* And about "the enemy" as you said, don't forget we are Europeans, not Anglo-Saxons and God's will may be to unite all Europe.

SOREL: With bayonets?

The Mayor doesn't reply but looks at him as if he deplored such a stubborn attitude. He bends over and looks at half a dozen worn volumes between bookends on Sorel's desk.

SOREL: *(continued) (before the Mayor can question them)* Those are my personal books.

MAYOR: *(inspecting titles, murmurs)* Juvenal . . . Voltaire . . . Plato . . . "The Republic" . . . *(looks at Sorel curiously)* My dear friend, we have to be careful about that word "republic."

Sorel looks out the window for a moment, his hands calmly folded behind his back. Then he turns very quietly to the Mayor who, feeling an unpleasant tension, picks up his hat to leave.

SOREL: Would you like to have my resignation?

MAYOR: *(at door, warmly)* By no means, by no means, my dear Sorel! We need you. You have the respect of the whole community. I only want you for your own good to understand our problems a little more clearly.

The hall door opens and we glimpse Albert and Louise. Albert is a little confused to find so important a person as the Mayor confronting him and he bows and stammers.

ALBERT: Oh, excuse me, Mr. Mayor—we were told that Professor Sorel—well, sir, I'm awfully sorry to intrude—

MAYOR: *(right over his stammering)* Come in, come ahead, Lory. I'm just leaving. Good morning, Miss Martin.

He goes out past them and Albert follows Louise into the room, still a bit off balance at confronting important authority. He bows to Sorel. Louise, who is devoted to old Sorel, looks at his face and sees something unpleasant has occurred. Sorel goes to his desk rather wearily.

LOUISE: *(with quick sympathy)* Is anything wrong?

SOREL: *(quietly)* Yes, Louise. Come here, please. Come here, Mr. Lory.

21

The three of them go to his desk and he opens a marked school-book on the desk top.
Close three shot—their heads bent over the book, the young girl, the middle-aged timid man and the strong-hearted old man. There is a sad smile on Sorel's face as he leafs open the book and puts his finger on a page which is marked for deletion.
SOREL: It's a very delicate surgical operation—to cut out the heart without killing the patient. The history of our country however is a very tough old patient, and we'll do the best we can. *(his finger moves on the book)* We start here, with Charlemagne . . .

INTERIOR SCHOOL—ALBERT'S CLASSROOM—DAY
There are about thirty-five desks in the room, which fronts on the street, but only about twenty boys aged ten to fourteen. One of the boys is Edmond Lorraine, who lives across the street from Lory above the department store. Edmond alone is sitting at his desk, studying, while the others are playing games, talking, stirring about noisily and, above all, watching the two oldest and most obstreperous boys, Julian Lamont and Henry Noble. Julian is drawing a caricature of Albert hugging and kissing Louise while Henry sets the hall door ajar, climbs on a stool and sets a box of chalk atop it so that when the door is pushed open the box will fall.
A small boy, something of a clown, is behind Albert's desk, imitating his shy awkward manner and wielding a long pointer in the direction of the pupils who are laughing. In the middle of their pranks the boy who is watching at the crack of the door makes a signal and they all fly to their desks.

INTERIOR SCHOOL—HALLWAY BETWEEN CLASS-ROOMS—DAY
From the further door of Sorel's office we see Albert and Louise come out with marked books under their arms, and we see Sorel close the door behind them. They come toward camera to door of Louise's classroom. Louise is full of sympathy for Sorel and indignant at what has been done to him. Before opening her door, while Albert looks at her with bashful love in his timid eyes, she turns to Albert, her voice low and indignant.

LOUISE: Why do they make us do this—this dirty work? Why don't they put in German teachers and be done with it?
ALBERT: *(trying in a blundering way to comfort her)* Don't—don't be upset, Louise. It's only a few pages.
Louise looks at him, suddenly very feminine and impatient with his clumsy blindness and lack of backbone.
LOUISE: Oh—*Albert!*
And she opens the door and goes into her class. We glimpse some of the little girls before the door closes sharply behind her in Albert's stricken face. He makes a vague gesture as if to follow her and then takes his hand quickly from the doorknob, and somewhat confused and vague turns to his own door at the opposite side of the narrow hall. But before the door he realizes where he is, and we suddenly realize by the effort he makes to gather himself together that it is always an ordeal for him to enter and face his boys. With exaggerated firmness he grasps the doorknob and tries to stride in commandingly, like a man who tenses his muscles before diving into cold water. The box of chalk falls with a crash in front of him, he jumps and spills the books under his arm, then stops rigidly while there is a guffaw of laughter which dwindles out into giggling as the boys watch him in malicious silence.

INTERIOR SCHOOL—ALBERT'S CLASSROOM—DAY
As Albert stoops to retrieve his spilled books, Edmond Lorraine springs forward to help him. Albert, with an effort at dignity, goes to his desk, and as Edmond goes back to his desk a larger boy sticks out a foot and trips him. Albert turns with a nervous jerk as the boy crashes, but Edmond quickly gets to his feet and slides into his desk without complaint. Albert is just about to put his books on his own desk when the blackboard catches his eye.
Close shot—caricature on blackboard—Albert hugging and kissing Louise and written crudely under it: "Teacher loves Teacher."
Close shot—Albert, as he looks at it with helpless horror, and we hear a repressed giggling from the boys.
Full shot. Albert, with the last vestiges of his dignity, quietly erases the caricature, but his hand trembles so that he finally drops the

23

eraser. Another giggle and he doesn't try to pick up the eraser, but sits down at his desk.

ALBERT: Until our new schoolbooks are supplied to us, we are going to make a few—corrections.

He looks at Edmond as being the only boy he can trust.

ALBERT: *(continued)* Edmond Lorraine will collect the pages after you have torn them out, and burn them in the stove. *(opens his book)* Page 7.

He tears it out, and we hear the ripping of twenty other pages as the boys obey simultaneously.

Close shot—Albert, as he turns to more pages. (The blackboard with the half-erased caricature behind him, we don't see the pupils.)

ALBERT: Pages 15, 16 and 17.

He tears them out together, and we hear the simultaneous ripping of the twenty boys with their books.

INTERIOR LOUISE'S CLASSROOM—DAY

Close shot of Louise in similar angle, the blackboard behind her. Her face is angry and rebellious, but she is firm and commanding as she turns to further pages of her own book.

LOUISE: Pages 21 and 22.

She tears them out and we hear the ripping of the other pages from the books of her class of girls.

LOUISE: *(continued)* Tear them out carefully. *(leafs to a further page which is marked for deletion)* Page 30. *(breaks off and looks up as we hear the whine of an air raid siren.*

Full shot—class, as a little girl squeals out nervously, hearing the rising whine of warning, as everyone freezes, listening.

LITTLE GIRL: It's the British!

LOUISE: *(her face lighting up)* Don't be nervous, Emilie, we have plenty of time. *(closes her book and stands up)* We must take shelter, even from our friends in the sky. As you pass out please give me the pages you have torn from your books—*(looks up as a nearer siren adds its scream to the first)* The time will come when we can paste them back where they belong.

24

*At her signal the girls form an orderly line. Louise goes to the hall
door and they start filing out, handing her the pages.*

INTERIOR SCHOOL—HALL BETWEEN CLASSROOMS—
DAY
*We see Louise at her door as the girls file out quietly and orderly.
Albert Lory stands by the opposite door of his own classroom from
which his boys are piling out pell-mell, noisily and disorderly.
The children are going down the stair at end of hall which leads to
the basement. We hear the warning sirens above the scuffling of
feet and the chatter of the boys. Professor Sorel comes along hall
and stops beside Albert, looks sharply at the disorderly rout of
boys.*
SOREL: Order, young men! Don't let the girls be better soldiers than
the men!
*Immediately the boys are quiet and keep in line like the girls. As
the last children pass the teachers, Albert, who is nervous, speaks
to Sorel who stands beside him watching the children pass down
the stair at end of hall a few yards away.*
ALBERT: *(over the sirens)* I—I'd like to get my mother. She's so—so
afraid of the raids.
SOREL: Go ahead, Mr. Lory.
*Albert hurriedly exits and Sorel goes the opposite direction,
following Louise who is herding her children down the stairs.*

INTERIOR SCHOOL BASEMENT—DAY
*Wide angle on children flocking down and finding places in the
low-ceiled, vaulted room which is dimly lighted. The stair is in left
foreground so that the children come down past camera, a little to
one side, and spread out as they look for places. There are benches
around the stone walls. Sirens less loud down here. The children
seem accustomed to this business and we hear their voices now as
they call to one another. In middle of cellar, at right, is another
door which leads up into an areaway near street. There are no
windows. Here and there electric bulbs hang from cords.*

25

EXTERIOR COURTYARD OUTSIDE SCHOOL—DAY
Albert emerges from school door and starts hurriedly for the gateway across yard. Camera pans on him as he increases his pace till he is almost running as he goes through the gate. (Sirens louder here.)

EXTERIOR CORNER OF FRENCH STREET—DAY
Shooting down sidewalk we see Albert hurrying toward camera. He keeps going faster until as he nears camera he is running. Camera pans as he rounds corner in front of camera and then stops abruptly, for he has almost collided with his mother who is coming the opposite direction in a brisk walk. He is so out of breath he cannot speak. His mother raises her voice above the growing din as she looks at him scoldingly. (This to be shot at ranch and if there are airplane noises it will not matter.)
MRS. LORY: Albert, what are you running for? Don't you know it's bad for your heart? Why aren't you in the shelter? Where's your hat?
ALBERT: *(panting, seizes her arm)* Hurry up, Mother! Hurry!
Camera pans back as they round the corner back toward the school which is down the street. Albert clutches her arm, trying to hurry her along. Sirens very loud now. They go faster, faster.

EXTERIOR SCHOOL COURTYARD—DAY
Shooting through gate into yard toward school building we see Albert and his mother come hurrying in from left and start across the yard for the main door of school. But suddenly above the screaming sirens we hear the sharp explosions of anti-aircraft guns and Albert, hanging to his mother's arm, dashes left toward a small door, jerks it open and frantically disappears inside. (This leads to the second and smaller basement door seen at right in the basement scene.)

INTERIOR SCHOOL BASEMENT—DAY
Full shot taking in the crowded grouped children. Louise and Sorel have got them all seated and in their places and have found seats themselves on separate benches. The anti-aircraft fire is increasing but it is more muffled down here, as is the sound of the

26

sirens. Suddenly above the growing muffled din there is a hard knocking at the small door at right. As it increases frantically, Sorel gets up and unbolts the door. As it swings open we see Albert and Mrs. Lory. (The door is very thick, like an icebox door, with a heavy bolt.) The noise is suddenly so loud that we cannot hear Sorel's greeting as he admits them. He closes and bolts the door behind them and returns to his bench, under an electric bulb, as Albert, still clinging to Mrs. Lory's arm, moves into the midst of the children, a bit wild-eyed. (Edmond Lorraine sits beside Sorel.) Close shot—Louise on bench at side. The little girl, Emilie, is on the end of the bench, beside her, helping hold the torn pages which Louise is sorting out and putting into a satchel. Louise looks past camera and calls out:

LOUISE: There's room over here, Mrs. Lory.

Wide angle as Mrs. Lory and Albert move through the crowded space to the bench where Louise sits, little girls on the floor around her feet.

Medium shot—Louise on bench as Mrs. Lory and Albert reach the bench. The thudding of anti-aircraft is increasing its muffled roar all the time. There are several old women and a couple of old men, one of them the school janitor, against the wall in background. Mrs. Lory sits down on the bench without paying any attention to Louise who moves over to make room, and Albert sits between them, next to Louise. Mrs. Lory notices this and after a moment's thought motions to her son.

MRS. LORY: Sit on this side, darling. There's a draft in this cellar. *(to Louise as he gets up obediently, still out of breath)* He catches cold easily. His lungs are weak.

Louise says nothing; she is busy sorting the pages which she has collected from her girls and putting them into the satchel. Albert sits down on the other side of his mother and Mrs. Lory gives Louise a triumphant look, which Louise takes no notice of. Now the anti-aircraft grows vicious and the air seems to thud in the cellar. Mingling with the gunfire we can hear the growling of the bombers.

Full shot—crowded cellar as everyone stops moving, listening and waiting. Sorel alone seems to take no notice, absorbed in his

27

*book which he is reading calmly under the one light. The oldest
and most unruly of Albert's boys, Julian Lamont, sings out:*
JULIAN: Now they're over us!
*Close shot—Julian and his companion in mischief, Henry Noble.
Both listening with the eagerness boys show for airplanes. Julian
begins to make the rhythmic growling in imitation of the air-
planes we hear, the boys trying to identify the kind of planes.*
HENRY: Four engines!
JULIAN: Wellingtons!
HENRY: No—Americans! Listen!
Now he *imitates the pulsing growling of the four-engine planes.
Medium shot—Louise, Mrs. Lory and Albert with others in
background. The uproar of anti-aircraft and planes very heavy
now and Albert seems to draw into himself, waiting tensely for an
explosion, sweat shining on his face, trying to control himself.
Suddenly we hear what he is waiting for—that creepy whistling of
a falling bomb, growing louder, then ending with a crump-thud in
the distance. Albert flinches. His mother puts an arm around him
comfortingly as she bursts out indignantly:*
MRS. LORY: It's outrageous—bombing innocent civilians! Why
don't they stay at home? Things are bad enough as they are!
LOUISE: *(looks up quietly from sorting her pages)* I wish I could see
the sky full of them, Mrs. Lory.
MRS. LORY: *(vehemently, accepting the open challenge)* Why don't
they bomb Germany, young woman?
LOUISE: Excuse me, Mrs. Lory, but have you noticed whose flag is
flying over our Town Hall?
*Close shot—Sorel. The little boy, Edmond, sits beside him with a
worried face. Sorel lifts his face from his book and looks at Louise
with a little smile. Then he returns to contemplation of:
Insert book in his hands. It is his beloved Juvenal and we mat
down to the line: "In order to preserve life, they lose the reason for
living."
Close shot—Sorel as he reads, ignoring the uproar of the air raid
outside.
Full shot as we hear the whistle of another bomb falling. Everyone
waits, motionless, and we hear the* crump-thud *nearer.*

Close shot—three boys of Albert's class, among them Julian and Henry. Julian nudges the others with a malicious grin and indicates off and they all look at:
Close shot—Albert and his mother. His mother tries to soothe him, as if he were still a small boy. Guns are pounding and planes growling overhead. There is another hair-raising whistle and a nearer explosion and Albert breaks, burying his face against his mother as she holds him in her arms.
Close shot on larger group of boys around the ringleaders, Julian and Henry. They are all looking at Albert and snickering and the little clown (who imitated Albert at his desk in the classroom) is giving an exaggerated imitation of Albert, throwing his arms around one of the other boys and shaking convulsively.
Close shot—Albert and Mother taking in Louise who now observes Albert's breakdown. Louise is comforting a little girl who is whimpering nervously as Louise draws her close.
Close shot—Sorel as he looks up from his Juvenal again and observes Albert.
Closeup—Louise as, distressed, she looks from Albert past camera at:
Close shot—Sorel, who shakes his head as if to say, "What a pity." Then he turns and looks past camera at:
Close shot—group of boys who are mocking Albert and laughing.
Close shot—Sorel as he looks severe and calls out sharply:
SOREL: *Young men!*
Close shot—group of boys as they instantly stop their skylarking. Full shot in cellar. The boys are quieted but now all the children are stealing glances toward the bench where Louise, Emilie, Albert and his mother are seated. Sorel has returned to reading his book.
Close shot—bench, taking in Albert and his mother, Louise and little Emilie. Louise realizes the children are watching Albert who flinches against his mother, unable to hide his fear as the antiaircraft gunfire increases and more bombs fall. As a near bomb whistles and crashes nearby Albert makes a choking sound and his mother tries to comfort him. Louise, glancing around unhappily and realizing the children are watching Albert, puts her arms

29

around Emilie who is beginning to whimper and cower close to her.

LOUISE: Now, now, Emilie, don't worry. There's nothing to be frightened of. *(raises her voice cheerfully)* We're quite safe here. It will soon be over now.

She gets up, taking the child by the hand as she moves among: Full shot as Louise moves into the midst of the children and calls out cheerfully:

LOUISE: Let's all sing. *(smiling as she gets their attention)* I believe if we all sing loud enough we won't even hear the guns. I know Julian Lamont has a strong voice. Come on, girls, don't let the boys sing louder than we do.

She starts a school song, motioning them all to join in, and soon the vaulted cellar is ringing with their voices, almost drowning out the pounding of guns and sounds of falling bombs, which are receding now.

Close shot—Albert and his mother. Over this the cheerful singing of the children. Albert slowly sits up and leans back, as the little boy, Edmond Lorraine, who alone is not singing, comes in hesitantly from one side and slides onto the bench beside his teacher.

DISSOLVE

INTERIOR SOREL'S OFFICE—DAY

Professor Sorel stands with his back to us, looking out the window but hardly seeing the few children who are running and shouting as they cross the courtyard homewards with their satchels. It is four in the afternoon. There is a timid knock at the door and, without turning, he calls "Come in."

Another angle taking in Sorel at window and the hall door as it opens hesitantly and Albert Lory looks in hesitantly, his hat in hand and some books under his arm, just as he was when he came to the school in the morning.

ALBERT: You—wished to see me, Professor Sorel?

SOREL: Yes, Mr. Lory.

30

Albert enters and shuts door behind him and we can see he is agitated. Sorel turns around to look at him, pitying him and wondering how he can begin, when Albert blurts out:

ALBERT: I know what you're going to say—I know I'm ridiculous. I'm stupid. I'm weak. I—I can't help it, sir. *(his voice trembles)* I'm a coward—

Sorel raises a hand as if to stop him but he is almost vehement in his agonized confession.

ALBERT: *(continued)* Yes, I'm a coward. I can't stand violence—it terrifies me. Noise—explosions—something happens to me. I'm a coward and I can't conceal it any longer from the boys—they see it— they saw it today—you saw it, sir. Even Miss Martin—*(his voice breaks and Sorel cuts in firmly)*

SOREL: Sit down, Mr. Lory. Sit down.

ALBERT: *(choking)* Now she knows I'm a coward.

He sits down heavily in the chair Sorel has indicated and stares miserably at the floor. Sorel studies him for a moment and speaks with quiet sympathy:

SOREL: Would you like to be transferred to a district where there are no air raids?

ALBERT: *(looks up in a panic)* No, no, no.

SOREL: Because of Miss Martin?

ALBERT: *(looks down at floor and just whispers)* Yes.

SOREL: Does she know how you feel?

ALBERT: *(shakes head and whispers—eyes on floor)* No.

SOREL: *(studying him)* I thought you were a confirmed bachelor like me.

Albert looks up at him.

SOREL: *(continued)* Oh, like all young men I fell in love, but—she died—and I found a great comfort in my work. *Our* work. My family became this school—my books, my teachers—you, Miss Martin— my pupils—*(smiles)*—many of them grown up now. *(very gravely)* You know it's a great thing to be a schoolmaster. It's a life work, Lory. You sacrifice a lot of things, but you get a lot in return. And now I believe we're the most important people in our country. It's a time for sacrifice now, more than ever—and our real happiness lies in our doing our job well. *(indicates the stack of verboten books on his desk*

31

ironically) Our Mayor was in here this morning talking about duty— but I prefer to use the word job. Those books must be burned. Very well, we must burn them.—We can't resist physically. But morally, within us, we can resist. We contain those books, we contain truth, and they can't destroy truth without destroying each and every one of us. We can keep truth alive if the children believe in us and follow our example. Children like to follow a leader—and they have two kinds of leaders today: We seem weak, we have no weapons, we don't march—except to air raid shelters—and our heroes are called criminals and shot against walls. The other leaders have guns, tanks, parades, uniforms, they teach violence, self-love, vanity, everything that appeals to the unformed minds of children—and their criminals are called heroes. That's a lot of competition for us, Lory. Love of liberty isn't glamorous to children. Respect for the human being isn't exciting. But there's one weapon they can't take away from us—and that's our dignity. It's going to be a fight—it is a fight, but if the children admire us they will follow us.

Through the open window we hear a muffled collision and then the sharp tooting of a locomotive whistle from the railroad terminal in the distance. Albert takes no notice, but Sorel looks up, then disregards it as he speaks to Albert with deep conviction.

SOREL: *(continued)* We will win, Lory—*(adds whimsically)*—or maybe we will get shot. But every one of us they execute wins a battle for our cause, because he dies a hero—*(smiles)*—and heroism is glamorous for the children.

Then he chuckles, seeing Albert's face illuminated by his words.

SOREL: *(continued)* I don't ask you to die, my friend. Not immediately. But if you think these things over I'm sure it will help you when—*(hesitates to mention air raids)*—when we are visited by our friends in the sky. *(very man-to-man)* Do you think you can handle your class and be less nervous next time?

ALBERT: Yes, sir. I'll try.

SOREL: *(pats his shoulder encouragingly)* Good. *(goes to his desk as the sounds in the street increase)* You should read the classics again, Lory. You'll find that at a time like this, they quiet the mind. *(selects one of his personal books from his desk, the book we saw him reading during the raid)* Here, take my Juvenal. Take it home with you.

32

ALBERT: *(rising to take it but glancing nervously at the window whence the sounds are rising)* Thank you, professor.

Now we hear the whine of a motor siren approaching swiftly along the street outside and Sorel, unable longer to ignore the rising uproar, steps to the open window and looks out into street.

EXTERIOR STREET—DAY

Close shot through window past Sorel. Two German soldiers on motorcycles go roaring past. Then a truck full of German soldiers bounces past. Albert has got to his feet and now he enters (from behind camera) beside Sorel. Through window past them we see two more motorcycles and then Von Keller's Mercedes tears past, Von Keller and Schwartz in the seat behind the soldier driver.

INTERIOR SOREL'S OFFICE—DAY

Full shot—room. Sorel and Albert looking out window and more noises of passing traffic as the oldest of the three printers whom we saw in the cellar (Durand, by name) enters from a side door carrying a small tool box in one hand. Stops short and calls to Sorel whose back is to him.

DURAND: Professor Sorel?

SOREL: *(turns as Albert keeps peering out window where we hear cars going past)* Oh, Durand. What's the trouble?

DURAND: *(looks at Sorel peculiarly)* There's been a wreck at the railroad yard. Supply train.

SOREL: Now it begins.

DURAND: *(deposits his tool box on desk as he replies)* I'm afraid so, sir. They'll take hostages even if it's an accident.

Durand takes a screw driver from his opened tool box and begins working on the desk lamp which is apparently burned out. Sorel turns to Albert still peering out window.

SOREL: Now we need to be strong, Lory.

He steps to the desk, casually opens the drawer, takes out several written sheets of paper, puts them in the tool box and closes it behind Albert's back. Durand continues working on the desk lamp, paying no attention to Sorel's action.

33

EXTERIOR RAILROAD TERMINAL—DAY—(STOCK)
Wrecked train. A locomotive on its side, steam hissing from it. A mess of piled-up freight cars (whatever we can find).

EXTERIOR RAILROAD—DAY
Wide angle on an overturned freight car. A pile of spilled packing cases are splintered and mashed alongside the tracks. German soldiers all around.
Camera pans down to close shot of broken packing cases and we see the destination stamped on it in big letters: BERLIN. It was full of eggs and half of them are spilled out and broken. A workman is helping clean up the mess. He looks up stealthily at a pair of German legs behind them and then slips a couple of eggs into his pocket.

INTERIOR SWITCH TOWER—DAY
Von Keller and his adjutant, Schwartz, are interrogating Paul Martin who stands by the row of big levers that control all the switches at the terminal. Through the big windows we see a maze of tracks and a few locomotives shunting around the yard. Two German soldiers stand just inside the door at the top of the iron stairway outside. The adjutant is taking notes as von Keller questions Paul, who is very calm and casual.
PAUL: I closed the switch at 4:17, according to the train dispatcher's orders.
VON KELLER: Show me the control.
Paul turns to the bank of levers and indicates one that is locked forward. (Schwartz, throughout all scenes where he is present, watches everything as if he were continually making mental notes.)
PAUL: This one, No. 14. I haven't touched it since.
VON KELLER: *(watching him keenly)* It seemed to operate all right?
PAUL: Yes, sir. As soon as I closed it I watched the freight backing into the terminal—that is, I expected it to go back. But instead it moved out on the main track just as the other train was coming in. It was too late to do anything.
VON KELLER: *(as adjutant makes notes)* See if it works now.

34

Paul unlocks the lever and it flops back and forth, freed of any pull. He looks astonished as von Keller watches his face closely.

PAUL: The control cable's broken.

VON KELLER: *(dryly) Cut.*

Paul stares at him.

VON KELLER: *(continued)* You knew nothing about it?

PAUL: No, sir. It was all right when I pulled it. I'm sure of that.

Von Keller turns away and stares out across the tracks, his hands behind his back.

VON KELLER: You turned in an illegal newspaper this morning.

PAUL: That's right, sir.

VON KELLER: Have you any idea where it comes from?

PAUL: No, sir.

VON KELLER: *(turns)* If you do get any idea, will you report it?

PAUL: I think so.

VON KELLER: *(makes a decision as he looks at him keenly)* Martin. This was an accident. You understand?

PAUL: Yes, sir.

Without a further word von Keller nods to his adjutant and they exit. One of the sentries follows and one remains. As the door closes behind them and they vanish, descending the iron stairway, Paul looks with a puzzled grin at the remaining soldier.

PAUL: *(continued)* What do you think, Otto? Am I in a jam?

SOLDIER: *(a friendly growl)* Nah—*(takes a pack of cigarettes from his pocket)* You smoke and forget it, Paul.

PAUL: Thanks. *(taking cigarette, still puzzled)* What's the old man up to? Why does he call it an accident?

OTTO: *(strikes match, gruffly)* We never ask questions.

EXTERIOR ROOM OUTSIDE GEORGE LAMBERT'S OF-FICE—DAY

(The door to the inner room is lettered: "Superintendent, Freight Terminal"). Wide angle as Julie Grant comes out of the door briskly with some typed papers in her hand. She meets Louise who comes hurrying in from opposite direction—toward George's door. Louise calls out anxiously as they stop for an instant.

LOUISE: Oh, Julie. Where's George?

JULIE: *(indicates door)* In his office. He's in an awful temper. *(catches Louise's arm and drops her voice anxiously)* I'm worried about Paul. I just saw that fat pig leave the switch tower. If the boss calls me, tell him I've gone to the warehouse.

LOUISE: *(with a trace of bitterness)* Oh, you don't need to worry about Paul.

She goes to the office door as Julie hurries on out.
Close shot of door with its lettering as Louise enters, very much perturbed.

INTERIOR GEORGE LAMBERT'S OFFICE—DAY
George, the superintendent, is behind his desk talking sharply into a desk phone as Louise hurriedly enters to him. Through window behind desk we can see the switch tower against the sky and the smoke of passing trains. Hear train noises. On wall beside window is a small cage, just a box with a wire screen cover at the front, through which we can see two pigeons in the box.

LOUISE: George—

GEORGE: Just a moment, dear—*(goes on into telephone)* No, no. Don't stop work. Go ahead and load No. 4. We'll have the tracks cleared within an hour. Speed it up, now. The men will have to work overtime... If there're any complaints refer them to me. That's right. Call me back as soon as you've finished.

He hangs up and rises to face Louise who has come anxiously to his desk.

GEORGE: *(continued)* I'm afraid I'm in for some trouble. Did you see the wreck? Everything's in a mess.

LOUISE: George, I'm worried.

GEORGE: So am I, dear. I don't understand how it happened. I've checked with Paul. Everything was all right at the switch tower. You know how hard I've worked to keep everything moving—but now the chances are they'll hold me accountable—

LOUISE: I'm sorry—perhaps I'm selfish—but I'm thinking about myself. Something's happened I don't understand.

GEORGE: *(comes out of thinking about himself and looks at her)* What, Louise?

36

LOUISE: I went out to get some things for our dinner tonight. I had to stand in line a long time, and when I got back the house had been searched. I'd put—

She breaks off as the door opens and Major von Keller enters with his adjutant, Schwartz. Louise gives von Keller a swift glance and her face goes cold as she looks away, pretending not to see him. George bows a little as von Keller comes over to the desk. (Schwartz just watches, and during scene eases over to George's desk and covertly scans the papers lying on it.)

VON KELLER: Excuse me, Lambert, if I'm intruding. I thought you were alone. You know my adjutant.

GEORGE: *(bows)* Yes, sir. I was expecting you. *(turns to the girl, inwardly proud to introduce her to a personage)* Louise, this is Major von Keller. Lieut. Schwartz . . . Miss Martin.

Von Keller bows gallantly and slips off his white glove to offer his hand but Louise looks at him coldly and ignores the hand, and he disguises his polite gesture by continuing the movement of his ungloved hand to his breast pocket, taking out his cigarette case as he smiles at her ironically. He directs his speech to George though he continues looking at the cold-faced girl.

VON KELLER: I know Miss Martin very well, even if she doesn't seem to know me. As protector of the town, it's my duty, Miss Martin, to know what our teachers are teaching—*(adds softly)*—and thinking. *(his smile deepens)* How are your "friends in the sky"?

Louise ignores him and turns to George quietly.

LOUISE: I wanted to see you alone. I can come back when you've finished.

VON KELLER: *(before she can move)* Go ahead, Miss Martin, don't mind me. *(to George, smiling)* She wants to ask you about some papers she's lost.

LOUISE: *(turns on him sharply accusing)* Not lost. They were stolen.

Schwartz smiles.

VON KELLER: *(his eyes twinkle)* My report to my superiors says neither. The forbidden pages were burned. *(very pleasantly)* You see we protect the people we like from their own mistakes.

GEORGE: *(anxiously)* What did you do, Louise?

37

VON KELLER: Nothing, Lambert. Nothing at all . . . except prove our efficiency.

LOUISE: *(coldly to George as she ignores the Germans)* I've found out what I wanted to ask you. I'll see you this evening.

And abruptly she exits past the Germans as if they were transparent. George is disturbed but as the door closes sharply behind Louise, von Keller turns to him blandly as if it were a closed incident.

VON KELLER: Don't be disturbed, Lambert. We have more important matters to discuss. I've just been making an investigation of the wreck. *(stares at George testingly)* A very unfortunate accident, Lambert.

GEORGE: *(grimly)* I wouldn't call it an accident, Major von Keller.

VON KELLER: *(dryly)* Neither would I. It was sabotage.

GEORGE: *(indignant about the matter)* I knew when they began circulating that illegal newspaper we'd have trouble. And this won't be the end of it.

VON KELLER: *(eyes him probingly)* Is there anyone you suspect?

GEORGE: *(bitterly)* I don't know. Who prints the newspaper? You can be sure every workman in the railroad yard gets hold of it. Find the men who print the newspapers and you'll find your saboteurs!

VON KELLER: *(dryly)* Very logical—but not very helpful. And not very intelligent for either of us to use the word sabotage.

GEORGE: *(protests bitterly)* But it *is* sabotage.

VON KELLER: You don't understand, my friend. If we call it sabotage I shall have to take hostages from the town—and shoot them finally if the guilty are not found. I don't like to shoot innocent people and I don't like to make martyrs—once you begin that it never stops until finally we'll find ourselves sitting on a powder keg. I've noticed what happens in our districts which we are protecting.

As George looks puzzled.

VON KELLER: *(continued)* Also the taking of hostages will only make the guilty men more cautious—and the shooting will make them more rebellious! Next time it will be a troop train that is wrecked. Fortunately, no German soldiers have been killed. Eggs, potatoes, meat—whatever's been destroyed by this—ah—accident can be replaced. The citizens in the town will eat a little less and *talk* a little

38

more. *You* can't be blamed for an accident—and meantime we keep our ears open. I have many ears, as you know, and you are in touch with all the men who work here.

GEORGE: *(bitterly)* You think they'll tell *me* anything? No. I'm the man who gives orders around here—and they regard anyone who gives orders as an enemy.

VON KELLER: *(nods thoughtfully)* I can remember the time when we had the same problem in Germany—during the Republic, under Capitalism. I fought in the streets for our Fuhrer, Lambert—I killed workers with my own hands. For my class it was either kill or be killed. But we won, and now we are brothers. Absolute obedience!

GEORGE: *(with bitterness)* I, too, fought the unions—right in this yard. *(shows a scar on his temple)* I was nearly killed. But you had a leader, and you were many. We had no leader and we were few. That's why you're here.

VON KELLER: But not as your enemy, Lambert.

GEORGE: If I thought you were I wouldn't be doing what I am.

VON KELLER: I know that. We're here to help men like you rebuild your own country. Remember what my country was before our Fuhrer. A country without food, without arms, without honor. But the people were not bad, they were only waiting to be told the truth. It's the glory of the Third Reich that we have shed German blood to give that truth not only to your people but to the Aryans of the whole world.

GEORGE: Your ideas are exactly my ideas. I saw how our country was destroyed. False democratic ideas—women refusing to have children—strikes in all our factories for a 40 hour week while your people were working 70 and 80 hours a week. I want the new order for my country. I work for it. But I know we can't have it till this war is over. I must tell you the truth—I don't like the Occupation.

VON KELLER: Neither do I.

George stares at him curiously.

VON KELLER: *(continued)* I'm glad we understand each other. We are both working for this war to be over. Only then can we have a peaceful and united Europe. And only then can your country—and men like you—regain their dignity and honor. *(extends his hand)* Let us both work for that day.

George grips his hand with emotion.

DISSOLVE

INTERIOR LORY HOUSE—DOWNSTAIRS ROOM—
NIGHT
*We see a very peaceful and very dull family scene. Albert and his
mother sit reading near the table lamp which sheds a soft glow
around them. Both are reading and both have shawls around their
shoulders, like two old women. From the house next door we hear
an accordion playing a charming love song. The music disturbs
Albert who raises his eyes from his book stealthily and glances at
his mother who is absorbed in the official newspaper, but a little
drowsy. His mother rustles the paper, perhaps turning a page or
straightening it so she can see better, and he quickly looks down at
his book again.*
*Insert book in his hands. We see it is the Juvenal which Sorel lent
to him that afternoon. Mat down to the same lines Sorel was
reading during the raid: "In order to preserve life, they lose the
reason for living."*
*Two shot as Albert ponders the page and then glances stealthily at
his mother again. She takes no notice, absorbed in her paper, and
cautiously he looks around, as if the music from next door were
drawing him. As he does so the newspaper slips from her hands
and rustles to the floor. Albert looks at her quickly, as if listening
off to the music were a guilty act, but sees she has fallen asleep. He
watches her a moment and then whispers to see if she is asleep.*
ALBERT: Mother.
*She doesn't stir and he looks around again in the direction of the
sentimental music next door, soft and charming music. After a
moment he watches his mother, then gets up very quietly and
cautiously.*
ALBERT: *(continued) (murmurs testingly again)* Mother?
*She is sound asleep and he softly puts down his book and takes the
shawl from his shoulders. He tiptoes, with many a backward
glance, to make sure his mother sleeps, to a side door which opens*

40

on a garden between the two houses—the Lory home and the Martins'.
Shot past him at the door. As he opens the door cautiously glancing back across his shoulder to make sure his mother doesn't see him, the music is louder and across the garden we see a lighted window. The glass is closed but the shutters are open. (No other lighted windows are visible because blackout regulations are enforced.) The music draws Albert, stronger than his fear of his mother, and after some hesitation he steps stealthily outside and closes the door very carefully, peering back at his mother through the closing crack.

EXTERIOR GARDEN—BETWEEN LORY AND MARTIN HOUSES—NIGHT
Close shot—Albert at side door. Still feeling guilty for what he is doing, he stands and looks around at the sky, like a man observing the night before he turns in. He knows he would still have an excuse if his mother should wake and call. He listens to the music. It is like a magnet and, taking his courage in his hands, he steps from the doorstep and goes across the garden furtively.
Camera follows Albert as he crosses the garden feeling like a burglar. The music grows louder as we approach the Martin house. A low fence between the two small gardens is an unexpected problem which makes him hesitate. Then like a man diving into cold water, he steps across it awkwardly. Music grows stronger. Camera follows him till he reaches the side of the Martin house and moves along it stealthily to the unshuttered window.

EXTERIOR MARTIN HOUSE—NIGHT
Close shot—Albert, camera a little behind him and on one side— as he furtively moves so that he can peer through the window. Music strong and sweet now, full of a feeling of love.

INTERIOR MARTIN HOUSE—NIGHT
Shot through window—what he sees: A charming scene of two pairs of lovers. Paul is stretched out in an easy chair playing the

*love song on his accordion, while Julie Grant sits on the arm of his
chair with her arm carelessly around his shoulder as she listens,
watching his face adoringly. Near them George Lambert and
Louise Martin are sitting on a small sofa and he is talking to her
as if nobody else were in the room, persuading her into something
obviously, though we cannot hear the sounds of their voices. We
see him take her hand and talk very urgently and masterfully and
she finally agrees, and he kisses her hand and gets up exultantly
and holds up his arms, waving his hands for Paul to stop playing.
As the music breaks off—*

EXTERIOR MARTIN HOUSE—NIGHT
*Closeup—Albert watching through window, the light from the
window across his face.*

INTERIOR MARTIN HOUSE—NIGHT
*Shot through window. We see George making an announcement
with elaborate pantomime and jokes we don't hear and then he
draws the flushed, laughing Louise up beside him, takes a ring
from his pocket and puts it on her engagement finger with a mock-
operatic manner and folds her in his arms as he kisses her. Julie
claps her hands excitedly and Paul, grinning, plays a wedding
march loudly and gaily on his accordion.*

EXTERIOR MARTIN HOUSE—NIGHT
*Closeup—Albert as he watches, a look of loneliness and torment
on his face. He is shut out from it all, it's like looking out from the
bars of a cage, the cage of his own stupid loneliness, at a happiness
which he knows he can never attain.*
*Close shot from behind Albert, past whose head we can see part of
the happy scene within. A hand comes in and grips his arm and he
starts fearfully.*
*Camera pulls back quickly to take in a policeman, who peers at
him and recognizes him. (The music and singing prevent their
voices being heard within.)*
POLICEMAN: *(growls)* Oh—Mr. Lory! What are you doing here?

ALBERT: *(stammering)* I—I—*(then he grabs at a straw as he indicates open shutters)* The shutters—open—I wanted to tell them . . . The blackout!

POLICEMAN: *(gruffly)* Oh, of course. I saw the light. That's what I came for.

He takes the shutters and closes them, blotting the happy scene from view. We hear a friendly miaow and Albert nervously stoops down and picks up Louise's cat. They are in dim light now.

POLICEMAN: Good night, Mr. Lory.

ALBERT: Good night.

Policeman watches him as he exits across the garden into darkness. Then as the music and singing continue within, the policeman stealthily pulls from his jacket a paper and starts slipping it under the shutters.

Closeup—policeman's hand pushing paper under shutters. As his hand moves away we see the word LIBERTY at the projecting top of the paper. The hand vanishes.

FADE OUT

FADE IN

EXTERIOR NEW YORK STREET—DAY

Close shot—down on curb in street—a stack of newspapers is flung on sidewalk just out of frame and some of them skid under lens and we see the word LIBERTY—it is a stack of the illegal newspapers.

Camera pans up quickly to wide angle on a cellar door between two shops on the street—the butcher shop at right with a queue of people lined up along sidewalk away from camera. We see that a German soldier has flung the papers out on the sidewalk and now a second soldier emerges from cellar and flings another stack of confiscated newspapers out on sidewalk. Half a dozen German soldiers with bayoneted guns form a cordon around the front of the place. There is a German truck guarded by soldiers drawn up at the curb. Now two German soldiers come up from the cellar lugging the small printing press which we saw in an earlier scene

43

and following them are two of the three printers whom we saw in the cellar printing the illegal newspaper. The two are Durand and a young man. The third man, middle-aged and with a face not easily forgotten, has evidently escaped or been out of the cellar when it was raided. (We shall presently see him in the watching crowd.) The two arrested printers have their hands up and are being herded by two German patrols with drawn pistols. The soldiers throw the small printing press into the truck as the two prisoners emerge from cellar, hands over their heads.

Medium shot—von Keller's Mercedes car parked across street. Mayor Manville and von Keller are in the back seat. The adjutant, Lieutenant Schwartz, is in the front seat beside the soldier driver. They are all watching silently past camera at:

Medium long shot of the scene described above. This shot takes in more of the queue before the butcher shop (from point of view of the car across the street) and we see the grim silent faces of the people watching the arrest. Near the head of the queue are Julie Grant and a little pot-bellied man whom we shall see during the story. Also the third printer, the middle-aged man with a face to remember. The two printers are herded toward the truck as soldiers pick up the illegal newspapers which had been flung out on sidewalk and throw them into the truck (where the printing press has already been heaved).

Near shot—taking in the two arrested printers and part of the queue in background. Now we can note Julie, the third printer, and the little pot-bellied man in the queue, watching. The printers have hands up, moving toward the truck, threatened by the guns of the patrols. Other soldiers move in, eyeing the crowd of onlookers. The policeman whom we saw with Albert in the previous fadeout pedals in on his bicycle, props it against curb and takes his place by the queue to keep order, apparently very much on the side of the Germans. Durand is a little slow in getting to the truck and one of the patrols gives him a shove, so that his hat falls off. Julie, before the soldiers can stop her, dashes out from the queue, retrieves the hat and puts it on Durand's head as he moves on to the truck at curb. One of the German soldiers politely but firmly takes Julie's arm and leads her back toward the queue.

Medium close shot—section of queue as the soldier brings Julie back to her place, just in front of the little pot-bellied man.

SOLDIER: *(with heavy accent)* So sorry, fraulein. You must keep in line.

The little pot-bellied man looks at the soldier with a deadpan and belches loudly. The soldier stares at him angrily and the little man touches his stomach with a polite and apologetic murmur.

LITTLE MAN: Indigestion.

As the soldier turns away he belches again. The soldier turns and scowls at him suspiciously but his face is innocent as he makes another apologetic gesture, and the soldier goes on out stiffly.

Close shot—von Keller and Mayor Manville watching from back seat of the Mercedes on opposite side.

Full shot—scene in front of cellar entrance and butcher shop. The people of the queue are hostilely watching the soldiers as they menace with their guns the two arrested printers who now stand in the truck with their hands in the air. The policeman stands with an eye on the queue. Suddenly the people of the queue begin to make a strange noise in unison without moving their lips— mmmMMMmmMMMmmmMMMmmm etc.—a sort of menacing murmur with a beat in it. The policeman, like a man who has to play the part of a good officer, shouts at them angrily:

POLICEMAN: *Quiet!*

The murmur almost dies away but we can still hear it from the silent row of unfriendly faces. The nearest people look at the policeman angrily as he walks along the queue. The sound keeps growing louder behind the policeman again.

Close on faces of von Keller and Mayor—in Mercedes car—who are watching past camera. (Manville has a copy of the illegal paper in his hand.) We hear that menacing murmur rising louder.

VON KELLER: *(softly)* The sound of the mob, Mr. Mayor. I don't like the way they look.

MAYOR: *(confidently)* You don't have to worry now, Major von Keller. Break up the printing presses and you break up rebellion. *(tears up the illegal paper scornfully)* This is the end of "Liberty."

VON KELLER: I hope so. *(to driver in German)* (Karl, go ahead.)

Manville throws the torn scraps of newspaper out of the car and it pulls out.

Camera holds as two German soldiers who have been waiting behind the commander's car follow the car, as a bodyguard.

Camera holds now on the vacated space and we see a citizen who has been lounging in a doorway at other side of sidewalk. He steps forward casually, drops his glasses by seeming accident and stoops to retrieve them.

Camera pans down to sidewalk and we see him pick up not only the glasses but the torn pieces of the illegal newspaper.

INTERIOR DARK ATTIC ROOM—DAY
Close shot of the back of a man. Stealthily he opens inward a small wooden door that covers an open window. Then he lifts in his hand a grenade, very close to camera.

Camera rises slowly and looks down past the head of the unknown man into the street below. We hear the whine of horn of the Mercedes car and see von Keller approaching to pass below with the two soldiers on motorcycles close behind. As the car is directly below, the hand holding grenade in front of camera flings the missile. Instantly the man turns to flee past camera and we recognize Paul Martin.

Long shot. We see the bomb miss the Mercedes car and explode with a shattering roar directly between the two motorcycle soldiers who are following. They are flung off their motorcycles.

Flash close shot—Mayor and von Keller—as they crouch in the rear seat of car to miss the blast, the mayor's hat blown off by the force of it.

Shot up street—Shooting across the two German soldiers who are sprawled beside the motorbikes, dead, as the Mercedes car tears up street away from camera with its siren going and we see half a dozen German soldiers come running around the corner into street.

EXTERIOR ROOF OF OLD BUILDING ON STREET—
DAY

Shooting down a stairway into an unused hall we see a man come pounding up toward camera. As he reaches top, right into camera, we see it is Paul. While he moves with all speed we see by his face he is not in a panic; he has thought out his whole plan beforehand. Camera pans as he dashes to right across the roof. There is a parapet and he is over it in a flash, disappearing from view. Below in the street we hear whistles blowing, shouts and noises of pursuit.

EXTERIOR STREET—DAY
Shooting down one side we see a dozen German soldiers running across and into various doorways to cut off escape of the fugitive. As far as we can see the soldiers are dashing into doorways. Whistles blowing and so forth.

EXTERIOR ROOFTOPS—DAY
Paul comes running toward camera, jumping from roof to roof as he approaches. As he reaches the roof of a fairly large building he runs into camera and stops short in close shot, looking past camera.
Reverse angle—what he sees—long shot across roofs and we see two German soldiers come up through a stairway and start toward camera.
Close shot—Paul—as he looks at the oncoming Germans, for once at his wits' ends. The Germans have moved faster than he anticipated.

EXTERIOR ANOTHER ROOFTOP—DAY
The one next to where Paul first ran to the roof. A German soldier appears over the parapet in close shot and then sees:

EXTERIOR ROOFTOPS—DAY
Long shot across roofs and we see Paul silhouetted against the sky on the further roof.

EXTERIOR ROOFTOP—DAY

Close shot—German—as he brings up his pistol and aims at the figure in the distance.

EXTERIOR LARGE ROOFTOP—DAY

Close shot—Paul, as he turns to look back whence he has come. We hear the shot of the German's pistol and Paul grabs his left arm. Paul looks around swiftly as he ducks low to get out of sight and camera pans as he runs in a stooped position to a large chimney at rear of the roof.

Large chimney on roof as Paul ducks behind it and crouches down looking for a way of escape. Finally his gaze fixes on a large window about twenty feet away, in the middle of the roof. He picks up a brick which has fallen from the crumbled chimney and waits, not visible to the oncoming soldiers so long as he stays behind the chimney.

Wide angle taking in both sides of the rooftop as the German soldiers come running from opposite directions. Paul lets fly with his brick and it crashes through the large dusty pane of the window, an instant before the soldiers jump over the parapets. The Germans look at each other for a split second, then all of them dive for the window and begin climbing through. As they vanish within, Paul straightens up and runs to the right.

INTERIOR LARGE EMPTY ROOM AT TOP OF BUILDING—DAY

The three German soldiers who jumped through the broken window are jerking open doors with drawn guns. Nobody there and they run down a stairway.

INTERIOR HALLWAY—DAY

The Germans come running down the stairway and jerk open the first door. We hear a woman's scream.

INTERIOR ROOM—DAY

A buxom woman stands in a small tin tub indignantly with a towel wrapped around her while the Germans, paying not the

slightest attention, are jerking open doors and overturning everything in the room. The next moment the soldiers are gone and the
room is in shambles.

EXTERIOR REAR OF BUILDING—DAY
A window opens, Paul comes out on a little balcony. A tree grows
beside the balcony. Paul springs with agility, catches a branch
and quickly lets himself down to the ground.

EXTERIOR SMALL BACKYARD—DAY
We are in a narrow space between two board fences. A sort of
small dingy garden. In a medium long shot we see three men
lurking silently behind a bush, as a gate opens in one fence and
Paul enters hurriedly, closing board gate behind him. Immediately the three men emerge from behind bush, and two of them
run to Paul as the third goes quickly to a closed gate in the
opposite fence. Paul is already jerking off his coat and we can see
his left shirt sleeve is reddened with blood. The two men have a
coat and a hat, the coat of a different color from the one Paul rips
off. One of the men slips on the other coat, the other gives Paul the
hat which he claps on as he starts for opposite gate, which the third
man has opened a crack so he can peer out. The first two men are
already exiting from whence they came as the third man nods to
Paul, lets him quickly out of the gate and closes gate and latches it
behind him. Evidently all this has been prearranged and it is
worked swiftly and silently, without a word.

EXTERIOR GARDEN AT REAR OF LORY HOUSE—DAY
Some wash hanging on the line. Paul enters quickly through the
rear gardens, gripping his left arm, glances around and sees no
one, starts for the rear of his own house next door. As he is passing
a sheet hung on the line, Mrs. Lory, who has just finished hanging
it there and still has a couple of clothespins in her mouth, comes
around and almost runs into him. He is startled but with presence
of mind he drops his wounded arm and smiles pleasantly at her as
he passes, as if it were an ordinary thing to walk through her
garden.

49

PAUL: Oh, hello, Mrs. Lory. *(goes on past nonchalantly)*
Close shot—Mrs. Lory—watching, a little curious and annoyed by his coming through her lettuce beds. She sees:
Medium long shot from her angle as Paul steps over the low fence (which Albert crossed the night before) and goes around to the back of his house and enters, vanishing.

EXTERIOR GATE OF GERMAN HEADQUARTERS—DAY
(This is in Notre Dame street, exterior Fleur de Lis, which will now have German flags and sentries in front of it.) A motorcycle shoots in and stops with a skid. (Sergeant Schneider on motorbike.)
Closer shot—in front of entrance. The German sergeant jumps off his motorbike and a soldier takes the machine as the sergeant starts to enter. He almost bumps into the little pot-bellied man who is passing on the sidewalk and the little man belches loudly. The little man puts his hand to his stomach and starts to murmur "Indigestion!" apologetically but the sergeant is in too much of a hurry even to notice it. Without expression the little man passes on innocently.

DISSOLVE

INTERIOR VON KELLER'S HEADQUARTERS—DAY
Mayor Manville stands uneasily watching von Keller, who seems not to have a care in the world as he is bent over an amusing little music box which is on his desk, tinkling out a dainty minuet while little mechanical figures dance atop of it. Lieutenant Schwartz sits behind his desk, back of which are filing cabinets, busily writing a report. (Through windows we can see into the great hallway of the castle where there is a bustling activity of officers and non-coms going up and down the stair.)
Close shot—Mayor watching uneasily at:
Close shot—von Keller bent over the little music box, apparently charmed by the gay music and the little dancing figures, as if he were oblivious of the mayor's agitation. Over the music we hear a

knock at the door. Von Keller calls pleasantly without looking around.

VON KELLER: Herein!

Close shot—heavy doors as they are opened from outside by an orderly and the sergeant, Schneider, steps in briskly and salutes. Full shot. Von Keller is still fooling with the music box, apparently absorbed in it, as he speaks in German to the sergeant.

VON KELLER: (What did you find, Schneider?)

SCHNEIDER: *(in German)* (The assassin got away, sir. They saw him but they didn't get near enough to recognize him. They fired several shots. Corporal Heinz is certain one of the shots took effect.)

Von Keller straightens up, looks at Schneider for an instant and then nods pleasantly.

VON KELLER: *(in German)* (Very stupid. You may go.)

The sergeant salutes and exits and von Keller shuts off the music box and sits on the edge of his desk, swinging a leg and staring at the uneasy Mayor a little grimly now.

VON KELLER: *(continued)* Well, that settles it. The man got away. Not even recognized. *(looks at the frightened Mayor with inward scorn)* This concerns you too, Mr. Mayor. An attempt was made upon your life as well as on mine.

The Mayor is silent before those steely eyes.

VON KELLER: *(continued)* Have you any suggestions?

MAYOR: What about the two men you arrested? They must know who it was.

Von Keller doesn't answer immediately. He picks up an issue of the illegal newspaper from a pile of them on his desk.

Close shot—von Keller, as he stares at the paper and we recognize it with the word LIBERTY across the top.

VON KELLER: I'm afraid you don't understand your own people. I know these men—*(taps the paper almost as if it were defying him)* We had them in Germany.

Full shot taking in von Keller as he looks up from the paper at the Mayor and adds grimly.

VON KELLER: Fanatics! They'll die—but they'll tell nothing. *(almost regretfully)* I'm afraid we'll have to take hostages. I don't like to begin

51

it, but—*(with a helpless gesture)*—two German soldiers have been killed.

MAYOR: *(unhappily)* I'm so sorry, Major von Keller.

VON KELLER: *(dryly)* I appreciate your sentiments, but this time my superiors won't accept any apologies.

Studies the paper in his hands, something revolving in the back of his keen mind.

VON KELLER: *(continued)* Have you ever studied this paper?

The Mayor is uncertain how to reply and he goes on musingly, as he reads an excerpt.

VON KELLER: *(continued)* "They make a desert, and they call it peace." Mmmm. Classical flavor. *(looks at Mayor)* Who wrote that?

MAYOR: Why, the men you arrested.

VON KELLER: Oh no, no, my dear Mayor, they were only printers. Workmen. They were the hands, I'm looking for the brain. This shows scholarship. *(turns to his writing adjutant)* Schwartz!

Schwartz looks up from his scratching.

VON KELLER: *(continued)* Give me that list of books you found on the desk of Professor Sorel.

Schwartz gets it out of a file and brings it over to him and he runs his eye down the list.

VON KELLER: *(continued)* Voltaire ... Plato ... Juvenal ... Tacitus—

That rings a bell in his memory and his face lights up.

VON KELLER: *(continued)* Tacitus! *(quotes the Latin)* "Ubi solitudinem faciunt, pacem appellant." *(points an excited finger at the blank-faced Mayor)* You recognize it, Manville?

MAYOR: *(hesitantly)* Is it Greek?

VON KELLER: *(his mind excited)* Latin! Tacitus is speaking of the Roman occupation: "They make a desert, and they call it peace." *(jubilantly gets up as he throws down the paper)* We've got it!

MAYOR: *(gets up agitated)* Surely you don't suspect my old friend Sorel. I've known Sorel all my life. He was always a little radical—he had crazy ideas—I never agreed with him—but he's one of the most respected men in the town. He'd never make an attempt on my life.

VON KELLER: *(in very good spirits now)* Of course not, of course not, my dear Manville. What about a glass of wine? We'll drink a toast to Tacitus.

52

The Mayor looks very relieved.

INTERIOR MARTIN HOUSE—DAY
Close shot—Paul Martin bent over the sink washing his arm. He has pulled off his shirt and is in his undershirt. We can see in this close shot that the wound is slight, just a flesh wound in his left forearm.
Camera pulls back slowly to take in a window that looks out on the street and we see Louise and Albert returning from the school. Albert is carrying her books like a schoolboy lover. They stop outside window (in front of door which we cannot see) and she takes the books from Albert and sees him looking at the ring on her finger. She laughs and we see her telling about the engagement as she shows him the ring. Then she turns into the house, vanishing from view. Albert remains standing, watching her with desperate expression even after the door closes behind her. He is awakened from his trance by Mr. Lorraine who comes along sidewalk holding the hand of his small son, Edmond. Albert starts as Lorraine speaks and then hurries on to his home next door. Lorraine looks after him curiously and then crosses street toward his place across the way.
Camera pulls back further to keep Paul in frame at the sink and also take in a door that leads into another room. Louise appears in the doorway taking off her hat. She sees Paul whose back is half to her as he is bent over the sink.
LOUISE: Paul—what's the matter?
Close shot—Paul, as he starts at sound of her voice and quickly grips his arm to cover the slight wound.
PAUL: *(casually)* Oh, nothing.
But she enters to him, sees he is hiding something, takes his hand and pulls it away from his left forearm.
PAUL: *(continued)* It's just a scratch.
LOUISE: *(looks at him, thunderstruck)* It was a bullet.
PAUL: *(still trying to pretend)* Don't be silly, Louise.
She stares at him incredulously, frightened, and a full realization floods into her face.
LOUISE: *It was you.*

53

PAUL: *(quietly)* I'm sorry you came in. I don't want you to get mixed up in anything. What you don't know can't hurt you.
Suddenly, unable to take her eyes from his worried face, she begins to cry.
PAUL: *(continued)* Don't do that. It's nothing, just a scratch.
For answer, still crying, she just puts her arms around him, choking for joy.
LOUISE: Oh Paul—I'm so happy. *(crying brokenly)* I thought—I thought—
PAUL: *(with great tenderness)* I know what you thought. Never mind.
She is unable to speak for her crying but she kisses him, clinging to him in pride and joy as we

FADE OUT

FADE IN

INTERIOR ALBERT'S CLASSROOM—DAY
It is early morning, just before Albert's arrival and the room is in an uproar. The two oldest boys, Julian Lamont and Henry Noble, are having a wild fox chase, dashing around after the slight boy, Edmond Lorraine, who is trying to evade them like a frantic rabbit. The rest of the boys are whooping it up and urging it on. Edmond is very agile but in trying to spring over a desk he trips and the two big boys pounce on him.
Close shot of the struggle on the floor. Edmond fights fiercely but they overpower him, pin his arms and legs to the floor. Then someone hands Julian an inkwell and he dips his finger in the ink and smears a "J" on Edmond's face.
Medium shot at hall door as it opens and Albert Lory steps in, his copybooks under his arm. Startled reaction as he sees:
Full shot. The boys have sighted the teacher and they scramble to their desks as fast as they can. Julian and Henry are the first to get behind their desks and Edmond is the last to get up and slide into his desk, blinking back his tears, the "J" still on his face. Albert musters a stern face and claps his hands at them sharply—and ineffectually.

54

ALBERT: Quiet, please! I'm very disappointed in you.

A loud miaow comes from somewhere though the boys sit very quiet. Albert's voice is kind, trying still to appeal to their hearts, which makes his failure the more absurd and touching.

ALBERT: *(continued)* This is a place of learning and culture, and the first requisite of culture is good manners—

Miaow, miaow, miaow—but he ignores them.

ALBERT: *(continued)* I've done my best to preserve dignity in this classroom, but if you continue to misbehave I shall have to report you to the Principal—

A chorus of derisive sounds from the boys. He looks at them helplessly and then his gaze fixes on Edmond who is trying to rub the "J" from his face with his sleeve but only succeeds in smearing it.

ALBERT: *(continued)* Edmond! What's on your face?

EDMOND: They say I'm a Jew.

ALBERT: Who did it?

As Edmond hesitates, scared—

Close shot—Julian Lamont. He slyly pulls back a rubber band and aims a paper wad.

Close shot—Edmond as the wet paper wad smacks against his cheek. He doesn't move.

EDMOND: I don't know, sir.

Close shot—Albert. His expression is somewhat like Edmond's. He has seen the paper wad but he knows he is up against something he cannot cope with.

Full shot as the rest of the boys wait to see what Albert is going to do. He motions to Edmond.

ALBERT: You may leave the room, Edmond. Go to the washroom and clean your face.

There is a snicker from the class as the little boy goes out of the room past Albert, but before the door can close, Louise appears in the doorway with a pale, excited face.

LOUISE: Mr. Lory! Come quickly! They're arresting Mr. Sorel!

For an instant Albert is thunderstruck. But as she vanishes he rushes out into the hall to follow her, his face shocked.

55

INTERIOR HALL BETWEEN CLASSROOMS—DAY
Shooting down hall we glimpse two German soldiers with Sorel between them turn the corner at end of hall to exit into street. Louise is running to overtake them and Albert runs ridiculously and madly after them to catch up, passing the little boy who is on the way to the washroom.

EXTERIOR IN COURTYARD ATTACHED TO SCHOOL—DAY
Full shot from gate which leads to street. In foreground is a military closed car, a German soldier behind the wheel. Across the court we see Lieutenant Schwartz waiting outside the school entrance, as two German soldiers emerge from the door with the calm-faced Sorel between them.
Near shot—doorway, as the soldiers come out with Sorel between them and start toward the car with Schwartz. The next instant Louise and Albert come running out behind them and Albert in his blind confusion and love for Sorel does the first brave act of his life. Frantically he grabs the arm of Sorel and hangs on to him, stopping him as he cries out:
ALBERT: Professor! Professor Sorel!
GERMAN SOLDIER: *(turns on him sharply, in German)* (Get away, you. Let go. Don't make any trouble.)
ALBERT: *(frantically and blindly, not even hearing him as he hangs on to Sorel)* They mustn't take you! Don't leave us! We can't run the school without you! The boys are getting out of hand! Don't leave us!
SOREL: *(reassuringly as the soldiers take hold of his arms to pull him away from Albert)* Dignity, Lory, dignity! You can run the school.
Albert grabs hold of the soldier who starts to pull Sorel along impatiently.
ALBERT: Stop it! Let go! You can't take him! I won't let you!
SOLDIER: *(angrily, in German)* (Shut up, you fool.)
And he gives him an angry shove. Albert goes back, his heels hit the step and he sits down with a hard thump, looking ridiculous.
Closeup—Lieutenant Schwartz as he looks significantly at:
Albert sprawled on step from his angle. Louise runs in to help Albert to his feet as the little boy, Edmond, runs out of the door to help his teacher.

56

Full shot as Schwartz nods to the soldiers and they quickly lead Sorel toward the car. Albert gets up, helped by Louise and Edmond.
Close shot—Edmond, Albert and Louise as they look past camera at:
Military car near gate. The soldiers are putting Sorel into a rear seat beside Mr. Lorraine. A guard stands on the running board.
Closeup—Edmond, a wild look on his young face as he cries out:
EDMOND: *Father!*
Wide angle taking in car, soldiers, Schwartz and the group in courtyard as Edmond runs to the car, calling to his father beside whom Sorel now seats himself calmly.
Medium shot—car, taking in soldiers and prisoners as the little boy tries to get on the running board and reach his father.
EDMOND: *(crying) Father! Father!*
Lorraine leans out, clasps him for an instant and kisses his son.
MR. LORRAINE: It's all right, son. Don't worry, I'll come back. You go home and comfort your mother. You're the man now.
The car pulls out, leaving the little boy standing there in the gateway. Louise comes to him, holding Albert's hand and leading him as if he were also a stunned child. With her free hand she takes hold of Edmond's hand, standing between the man and the boy as they look after the car which we hear going down street out of scene. Both Albert and Edmond are crying silently but Louise is strong, ready for the fight.
LOUISE: You're a brave boy, Edmond—
Then she looks at Albert and on an impulse kisses his cheek as she would kiss a child.
LOUISE: *(continued)* And so are you, Albert.

DISSOLVE

INTERIOR VON KELLER'S HEADQUARTERS—DAY
Von Keller sits behind his desk, a glass of wine in hand, looking quizzically at Louise, who sits stiff and angry in an ornate chair, an untouched glass of wine on a small table beside her. Von Keller sips his wine and sets down the glass with polite finality.

VON KELLER: I'm afraid you're wasting your time, Miss Martin. And mine too.

He reaches out and turns on the little music box and the minuet tinkles softly as the little mechanical figures dance or revolve. Louise doesn't know what to say but she finds this attitude hard to stand. Her eyes flash angrily as she finally bursts out:

LOUISE: Surely you can't have anything against Professor Sorel. Everyone in town knows him and respects him. A lot of us love him. He's a fine man—a good man.

VON KELLER: *(dryly)* And he writes very well. I admire his style.

LOUISE: *(not understanding his subtlety; pleading)* He's a kind man. You ought to know he wouldn't do anything violent. And Mr. Lorraine—

VON KELLER: *(cuts in sharply)*—Is a Jew.

He reaches out abruptly and cuts off the music box. Louise watches him, a little frightened.

LOUISE: What will happen to them?

Von Keller gets up and goes to her, framing his reply.

Closer two shot as he stops in front of her chair, studying her, his voice quiet.

VON KELLER: Miss Martin, two German soldiers were murdered today—out there in the street. If the criminal does not give himself up within a week, ten hostages will be shot—

She flinches and he adds quickly:

VON KELLER: *(continued)*—But not by me. Their deaths will be caused by the cowardice of the criminal who refuses to confess his guilt.

LOUISE: *(looks at him with horror)* You'd shoot innocent men?

VON KELLER: I told you I have nothing to do with it. But I confess I don't find myself grieving for the innocence of Sorel. Your own hostility to me reflects his teaching. And you pass it on to your children. These ideas are a contagion and the place to stamp them out is in the schools. You can make a child believe whatever you want, and the children of today are the soldiers and mothers of tomorrow. Ten years ago our German children were like yours. But we National Socialists threw out the Sorels and took charge of the schools—and look at them now: heroes who have conquered the world.

58

LOUISE: *(gets up in horror)* No, no. You never can.

VON KELLER: *(looks at her amusedly for a moment)* My dear child, if I didn't know you were going to be married to a very reliable man I'd be worried about you.

She looks at him with silent loathing and he smiles.

VON KELLER: *(continued)* You prove by this childish outburst how infallible our Fuhrer is in confining women to motherhood and home.

LOUISE: *(coldly, now in possession of herself)* Thank you, Major von Keller, for helping me to understand what this Occupation really means.

VON KELLER: *(as she turns to the door)* Thank you for your company, Miss Martin. And don't worry too much about Sorel—we have ways of finding out things—the chances are we'll find the guilty man. *(chuckles as she exits)* My regards to Lambert—and save me a piece of the wedding cake.

DISSOLVE

INTERIOR GEORGE LAMBERT'S OFFICE—AT FREIGHT TERMINAL—DAY

George is busy at his desk, and through the big window behind him we see freights shunting on the maze of tracks and the switch tower beyond, as the door opens and Louise enters, disturbed by her encounter with von Keller.

LOUISE: George!

GEORGE: *(gets up eagerly)* Darling, this is a surprise.

He looks to see that no one is passing window and then puts his arms around her and kisses her.

GEORGE: *(continued)* No school today?

LOUISE: *(suddenly very feminine, she wants to cry on his shoulder)* They arrested Professor Sorel.

She begins crying and he holds her close to him and comforts her tenderly and sympathetically.

GEORGE: Poor darling. Don't cry. *(kisses her)* Come, sit down, dear. I know how you feel. Crying won't do any good.

59

He leads her over to his chair and she sinks into it, glad to be weak for a change and have someone to comfort her. He takes his handkerchief and dries her eyes.

GEORGE: *(continued) (as to a child, tenderly)* There now, is that better?

LOUISE: George, I'm frightened. I'm scared to death. Life is getting horrible. I don't know what to do. I need you.

GEORGE: Of course you need me, darling. That's what I'm here for. I love you.

As she relaxes, comforted:

GEORGE: *(continued)* I know all about Sorel. They also took that fellow that runs the store across the street from you—Lorraine, and eight other men. One of them worked here in the yard. *(petting her comfortingly)* But nothing can happen for a week. If they find the man who threw the bomb they'll all be released.

LOUISE: *(half out of her mind)* But that's just it. You don't understand. The man who threw the bomb—Oh, George, I'm in an awful situation.

GEORGE: *(comfortingly)* I know, dear, I know. The man who threw the bomb is a criminal.

Louise draws back and looks up at him as if she couldn't have heard right but in his indignation he doesn't notice it.

GEORGE: *(continued)* If he has a spark of courage he'll come forward and admit his guilt—save innocent men.

LOUISE: *(staring at him)* You really think he's a criminal?

GEORGE: *(righteously)* Look, Louise, all of us hate this Occupation. I stood up to Major von Keller and told him to his face I didn't like it. But we have to face facts: They have the power. If one of us wants to resist, and get killed, that's foolish but courageous. He takes the risk and punishment himself. But the man who secretly resists, with acts of sabotage, is a coward; he escapes and innocent people die.

LOUISE: *(staring at him)* You believe that?

GEORGE: It's obvious, darling.

LOUISE: *(looking at him strangely)* You mean everyone who resists the enemy should give himself up, George?

GEORGE: I think so.

LOUISE: Then there is no more resistance.

GEORGE: Then we'd have peace. Wouldn't we be better off? Our duty now is to keep alive. To exist. What becomes of a nation if its citizens all die? Do you want to die? Do I want to die?

LOUISE: *(quietly; looks at him as if she had never seen him before)* I saw them take Professor Sorel. He's not afraid to die.

She gets up and looks out the window, suddenly a million miles from him.

GEORGE: But he's old. We're young. Life means everything to us.

LOUISE: *(looking out at the switch tower)* I know young men who aren't afraid to die.

GEORGE: *(goes to her)* Nothing is worth the sacrifice of your life, Louise. We have everything ahead of us—love, marriage, children—

LOUISE: *(turns on him)* No, George.

He looks at her blankly as she takes off the ring and drops it on his desk.

LOUISE: *(continued)* I was in love with you. Maybe I'm still in love with you. But I begin to feel as if I'd never looked at you before. This is the first time you've been frank with me. My mind's confused—I haven't the right answer yet for the things you've said, but I feel—I *know* you're wrong.

Her eyes widen as the door swings open and Paul walks in, his usual gay self.

PAUL: Hello, folks. *(grins)* I don't know how you do it, George. I can't get my girl to come down here and visit me.

Louise walks straight past him and exits. He looks after her curiously, then at the discomfited George.

PAUL: *(continued)* Hey, what's the matter?

GEORGE: *(trying to cover up, hiding the ring in his hand)* Oh, she's just upset. She'll get over it. You know women.

PAUL: *(laughs)* I sure don't.

FADE OUT

FADE IN

EXTERIOR MEADOWLAND OUTSIDE THE TOWN—DAY—(LOCATION)

Long shot. Two tiny figures, a man and a boy, appear against the bright sky over a rise of ground in the distance, coming toward camera. (Doubles)

DISSOLVE

EXTERIOR MEADOW—DAY—(STEREO & PROCESS)
Near shot and we recognize the two figures as Albert Lory and Edmond Lorraine. The time is several days later. They are picking flowers in the meadow as they come toward camera, stooping here and there. Suddenly Edmond sees some flowers very near camera and he runs to them.

EDMOND: Mr. Lory! Look!

Albert follows him and camera pans down to close two shot as they pick the flowers, Albert arranging the growing bouquet in his hands rather fussily. The little boy arranges his own bouquet and suddenly his face goes grave as he looks at them.

EDMOND: *(continued)* I wish I could take these to my father.

Looks up at Albert who is silent, arranging his own flowers.

EDMOND: *(continued)* Mama says they'll let him go. Maybe the end of the week. *(then worried)* But last night she was crying.

ALBERT: *(man to man)* You tell her not to worry, Edmond. They'll find the guilty man.

EDMOND: *(picking another flower gravely)* I hate to leave you, Mr. Lory.

ALBERT: *(looks up)* What do you mean?

Camera follows them as they move along, picking more flowers.

EDMOND: Mama says they're going to send us away to Poland. But I don't care—if we're with my father. *(then as an afterthought)* Some day we'll come back and see you again—you and Miss Martin. *(looks up artlessly)* Are you going to marry her, Mr. Lory?

ALBERT: *(almost drops his flowers, very embarrassed before the candid gaze)* What an idea! Don't you think I'm too old for her?

EDMOND: Are you old, Mr. Lory?

ALBERT: *(fussed)* Well—uh—I'm not—uh—I'm not as young as Miss Martin.

EDMOND: *(innocently)* Are you older than Mr. Lambert?

62

ALBERT: Yes.

EDMOND: *(trying to fix things)* But now she doesn't want him. Maybe it's because he's too young. She liked Professor Sorel and he's old.

ALBERT: Edmond, I'll tell you something. Women are hard to understand.

Another angle on them—Shooting across the water close on Albert as he leans out to pick an overhanging flower, the boy just behind him. There is a dreamy look in Albert's eye as he sees something in the water just under low camera.

What he sees. Closeup his own face reflected in the water. Into it comes his dream and we see Louise's face reflected as she kisses him on the cheek, just as she did after the soldiers took Mr. Sorel.

Close shot—Albert looking dreamily at the reflection and smiling a little as Edmond leans over to look curiously.

EDMOND: You see a fish, Mr. Lory?

ALBERT: *(studying his reflection, very seriously)* Do you know what it is to be in love, Edmond?

EDMOND: Yes, sir. I love my mother. And Miss Martin, too.

Albert looks at him as if he were a man and both sit down on the grassy bank.

ALBERT: You're very young, but maybe what I'm going to tell you now will help you some day when you're old. First, remember this— the most wonderful thing in the world is to love somebody.

The boy listens attentively.

ALBERT: *(continued)* Second, women are a mystery. You never know how they feel toward you. You think there's no hope—that they're going to marry someone else—and suddenly you get a kiss and they break with the other man. You must never despair, no matter how old you are. *(confidentially)* And now she's invited me to dinner. That brings up another problem—your mother. Your mother loves you, but for some reason she doesn't like other women. You've got to be firm—*(sighs)* It's not easy, Edmond.

EDMOND: *(very interested)* My mama likes Miss Martin.

ALBERT: Wait till you grow up. *(very puzzled himself)* The last problem is how to declare your love. A little gift—flowers—they help. Remember that.

EDMOND: Yes, sir.

ALBERT: *(glances around to make sure they are alone)* You stand up and I'll show you how it's done.

Both get up, the boy profoundly interested in the role he is enacting.

Medium two shot as Albert bows to the boy and presents his bouquet.

ALBERT: *(with confidence)* Please accept these poor flowers as a token of my admiration and love—

DISSOLVE OUT

DISSOLVE IN

INTERIOR MARTIN HOUSE—DINING ROOM—NIGHT

Albert and Louise sit facing each other across the little table. A lamp sheds a soft glow on their faces. Three places are laid, but Paul has not yet come home, even though the dinner is finished. (The cat is in this scene.) Albert is very shy and self-conscious, ill at ease in contrast from his confidence with the little boy. There is silence as Louise pours coffee into his cup and then into her own, glancing anxiously at Paul's unused plate and empty chair as she sets down the coffee pot. There are beads of sweat on Albert's forehead as he summons all his courage and begins:

ALBERT: Louise, I—there's something I wish to say to you. *(adds a little desperately)* Something important.

LOUISE: What?

ALBERT: *(looks at her desperately, then blurts)* This coffee is excellent.

LOUISE: *(looks at him as if she thinks he has suddenly lost his mind)* It's not real coffee, Albert.

ALBERT: *(with a mighty effort)* It's—it's better.

LOUISE: *(still thinking his conduct strange)* I've almost forgotten what coffee tastes like. This is made with roasted corn.

ALBERT: I—I wouldn't have known it.

LOUISE: *(looks at him closely)* You feel all right, Albert?

64

ALBERT: *(puts his fingers to his collar rather feverishly)* It's a little warm.

LOUISE: I'll open the window.

Albert watches her helplessly as she goes to the window, opening the glass but leaving the shutters closed, so the air can circulate through it without showing light outside. As she comes back to table she looks anxiously at Paul's unused plate.

LOUISE: *(continued)* I don't understand why Paul isn't here. He knew you were coming for dinner.

ALBERT: *(gets to his feet, looking at her glassy-eyed)* Louise, I have something to say to you.

LOUISE: *(looks at him closely, realizing he's not normal)* Albert, are you worried about something? Is it your mother? I know she doesn't like me. I know she didn't want you to come here.

ALBERT: *(in helpless protest)* I—

LOUISE: *(sweetly)* Don't apologize, you don't have to explain a thing. She's old and lonely. I understand how you feel. You go now—you don't have to stay any longer.

ALBERT: *(like a drowning man)* Thank you, Louise.

He goes toward the door, too incoherent to explain, and she calls out.

LOUISE: You forgot something.

She gets a package wrapped in tissue paper and takes it to him. Albert at door as she comes to him with the package. He looks at her desperately.

ALBERT: It's for you.

LOUISE: *(surprised)* For *me?*

She opens the paper and we see the bunch of wild flowers he picked with Edmond during the afternoon.

LOUISE: *(continued)* Why, they're lovely. Where'd you get them?

ALBERT: Edmond—uh—picked them for you. You know he's—uh—very fond of you. *(then blurts out)* Louise—Louise—I must speak to you—Louise, I know I'm not young—and you're so young in mind—I remember the day you graduated—I was already teaching then—

She is looking at him wonderingly as he struggles on desperately.

65

ALBERT: *(continued)*—and the day you came back to teach your first class—I was worried about you, and so happy when I saw how the children loved you—*(takes her hand)* And now we're both here together—we're the only ones left in the school—I feel so close to you—

There is a shattering explosion in the distance that shakes the windows, and he breaks off, both startled.

LOUISE: What's that?

There is a second explosion, and then a third, reverberating.

INTERIOR LORY HOUSE—NEXT DOOR—NIGHT
Mrs. Lory, who has been reading the newspaper beside the lamp on the table, has got to her feet with a startled expression. As she listens we hear another reverberation in the distance. She quickly puts out the light and hurries to the front door, opens it a crack and peers out into the dark street. We hear the rising whine of a siren in the distance. Mrs. Lory shuts the door and hurries to the side door that opens on the gardens between the two houses, thinking of her son Albert.

EXTERIOR LORY HOUSE—SIDE DOOR—NIGHT
Close shot on Mrs. Lory as she opens the door and peers out into darkness. She hears what we do, running feet approaching. As she watches:

EXTERIOR GARDEN BETWEEN HOUSES—NIGHT
What she sees: A dark figure comes running across the gardens behind the row of houses, jumps the fence and the next instant we see an oblong of light as the shutters of the Martin house are pulled open.

EXTERIOR MARTIN HOUSE—NIGHT
Close shot—window of Martin house. We see it is Paul Martin who is climbing into window.

EXTERIOR LORY HOUSE—NIGHT
Closeup—Mrs. Lory, watching from her doorway.

INTERIOR MARTIN HOUSE—NIGHT
Louise and Albert look dumbfounded as Paul scrambles in through the window, closes shutters behind him. Louise runs to him in a fright, understanding everything now in a flash.
LOUISE: *Paul!*
PAUL: *(closes window swiftly)* Lock the door, Louise!
Paul turns, seeing the frightened Albert but making no explanations.
PAUL: *(continued)* Lory! Sit down at the table!

EXTERIOR LORY HOUSE—NIGHT
Close shot—Mrs. Lory peering out half-opened door. We hear police whistles coming nearer and more sirens of the German soldiers. A motorcycle races through the street on the other side of the house. Now we hear voices and men and she sees:

INTERIOR LORY HOUSE—NIGHT
Shot through half-open door. Half a dozen German soldiers are coming through the garden with flashlights, going toward the Martin house next door. The door is closed softly by Mrs. Lory, blotting them from view, though we still hear their German voices and whistles.

INTERIOR MARTIN HOUSE—NIGHT
Three shot at table—Paul, Louise and a frightened Albert. Louise is smearing Paul's plate to make it appear used, as Paul lights a cigarette and offers one to Albert, speaking in a sharp, low voice. (Whistles and voices approaching.)
PAUL: Understand. I was here for dinner. I've been here for an hour. *(impatiently)* Smoke it, man. Smoke it.
ALBERT. *(fumbling with the cigarette)* I don't smoke.
PAUL: *(thrusts lighted match at its tip)* Breathe in.
There is a hard knocking at the door as Albert does so, chokes on the smoke and begins to cough helplessly. Paul pays no attention but motions to Louise and she gets up and unlocks the door. As she opens it a German sergeant steps in followed by two soldiers. We see more soldiers outside the door. The sergeant looks at

67

Albert coughing and Paul gets up nonchalantly from the table, cigarette in hand.

PAUL: *(continued)* Hello, sergeant. What's the trouble? What were those explosions?

SERGEANT: Ammunition train!

He looks around room suspiciously as the two soldiers open other doors, looking around.

SERGEANT: *(continued)* Anyone come in here?

PAUL: No.

SERGEANT: *(points at the coughing Albert who holds his cigarette like an amateur)* You live here?

Albert shakes his head, coughing, his face pale and sweating.

SERGEANT: *(continued)* What are you doing here, then?

LOUISE: *(as Albert coughs)* He's Mr. Lory from next door. He was having dinner with us.

SERGEANT: *(now confronting Albert who is still coughing, tears running from his eyes)* Why don't you answer when you're spoken to?

ALBERT: *(holding up cigarette—incoherently)* I don't—*(coughs)*—smoke.

Louise looks frightened but Paul covers it with a laugh to the sergeant.

PAUL: He's the schoolmaster. I gave him his first cigarette.

The sergeant, contemptuous of the jellyfish Albert, takes the cigarette from his shaking fingers and throws it on the floor.

SERGEANT: How long you been here?

ALBERT: Oh—I came home with my mother—and then I read the—

SERGEANT: *(impatiently)* What time?

ALBERT: *(swallows)* Six o'clock.

SERGEANT: Who was here?

ALBERT: Why, Louise—I mean Miss Martin—and—and—

LOUISE: *(quickly)* And my brother Paul.

SERGEANT: *(sternly to her)* I'm not asking you. *(to Albert)* Who was here?

ALBERT: *(pointing at Paul and finding it hard to lie)* He was here.

SERGEANT: *(suspiciously)* You're sure about that?

ALBERT: *(shakily)* Yes, sir.

SERGEANT: *(turns on Paul, indicating Albert)* And you're sure this old fellow was here all the time?

PAUL: *(grins)* Sure, sergeant. He's sweet on my sister.

The sergeant looks at Louise, then at Albert, then says in German to the two soldiers who have returned from searching the other rooms: ("In the old pans, they make the best soup") The soldiers laugh, looking at Albert. But even as they laugh, Mrs. Lory, very angry and indignant, comes running to the open door, pushes the soldiers aside and confronts the sergeant, her voice high and furious:

MRS. LORY: You get those men out of my house! Where do you think you are—in Germany?

SERGEANT: Please, please, lady—

MRS. LORY: *(right over his protest, seizing his coat sleeve and pulling him toward door)* Don't give me any please—please—You get them out of my house! I'm a decent, law-abiding woman, and I don't hide anybody! *(shoots an angry look at Louise)* I don't hide anybody! *(then to sergeant)* You've got no right to come banging into my house. *(over her shoulder, sharply)* Albert! You come home!

ALBERT: *(suddenly remembering the illegal newspaper hidden in his room and terrified at the idea of the Germans finding it in their search)* Yes, mother. *(follows her hurriedly)*

INTERIOR LORY HOME—DOWNSTAIRS ROOM—NIGHT
Full shot. Everything is topsy-turvy in the room, and we hear a heavy-footed German soldier clumping down the wooden steps from upstairs. Then he appears, a beefy, hulking fellow, looks around like a man doing his duty thoroughly, sees one cupboard unopened, goes over and jerks open the door as if he expected to find somebody hiding there. Mrs. Lory's pride, a set of old china, tumbles from the shelf atop the cupboard and crashes on the floor, just as Mrs. Lory comes running in, followed by the sergeant and the alarmed Albert. Mrs. Lory explodes with fury.

MRS. LORY: Oh, my stars—my best china! *(yells at the sergeant as she points at the littered fragments)* My wedding gift from the mayor!

(yells at the beefy soldier who blinks, taken aback) Get out of here, you lummox!
SERGEANT: *(stares at the beefy soldier; in sharp German)* (Come here, Timmermeister.)
> *The beefy soldier steps over in front of him smartly, and the sergeant gives him a terrific smack across the face. The man blinks and doesn't move though tears come to his eyes. Albert flinches at the brutality of the act and even Mrs. Lory is startled. The sergeant turns very politely to Mrs. Lory, as if he had proved the correctness of Nazi behaviour.*
SERGEANT: *(continued)* Are you satisfied, lady?
MRS. LORY: *(indignantly)* No! You're a brute! You're all brutes!
> *The sergeant stares at her uncomprehendingly, thinking he must be dealing with an insane woman, and utterly at a loss to know what to do, as we*

FADE OUT

FADE IN

INTERIOR LORY HOUSE—NEXT MORNING
> *The breakfast table is set, the official newspaper propped up in front of Albert's chair. We hear his clump down the stairs and he appears with Louise's cat in his arms, stops mechanically at the tall clock at the foot of stairway and sets it back five minutes, from 7:35 to 7:30. Through the door we can glimpse Mrs. Lory in the kitchen preparing his coffee. Albert goes to front door to put the cat out but something catches his eye.*
> *What he sees: A small newspaper half under the rug where it has been surreptitiously slid under door during the night. Albert stoops into frame, puts cat on floor and picks up the newspaper with a startled face.*
> *Close shot—Albert as he straightens up to examine the paper. It is smaller and more badly printed than the first illegal paper, not much larger than a letterhead, but across the top we see the word LIBERTY. Albert peers at it incredulously.*

70

Insert newspaper—set in bad type: Under the caption "LIB-ERTY" we see the headline "WE HAVE HEROES IN THE TOWN."
Medium shot—Albert, as his face lights up, scanning the paper. From the kitchen we hear his mother call:
MRS. LORY'S VOICE: Albert?
Albert swiftly folds the paper and puts it furtively in his inside coat pocket.
ALBERT: Yes, Mother.
Now she appears from the kitchen with the coffee pot in hand.
MRS. LORY: Sit down, darling, you'll be late.
He sits down and picks up the official newspaper as she grumbles, pouring his coffee.
MRS. LORY: *(continued)* They ought to be ashamed to call this coffee. Nothing but burned corn, and you have to stand in line all day to get four ounces of it. I'd like to see what the Mayor has on his table. I'm sure it's not this.
There is a yowl from under the table as she treads on the cat and jumps.
MRS. LORY: *(continued)* Oh, that filthy cat! I wish you wouldn't let it in the window every morning.
ALBERT: *(timidly)* It's a very nice cat, Mother.
MRS. LORY: *(impatiently)* Albert, you'll never grow up.
Albert is answering mechanically and looking at the newspaper to which we cut as their voices continue:
Insert official newspaper: Its caption is:
"VOICE OF THE PEOPLE"
(Passed by Official Censor)
SABOTAGE!
"Four German soldiers, all heads of families, were killed last night in the explosions which destroyed a trainload of munitions. Mayor Manville was summoned to the headquarters of Major Erich von Keller, Protector of the Town, and notified that such criminal acts will have grave consequences for the civilian population."

71

ALBERT'S VOICE: *(over insert)* How's your rheumatism this morning, Mother?

MRS. LORY'S VOICE: I had to get up in the middle of the night and rub my legs with liniment. I think I must have caught cold while I was sitting up waiting for you to come home. You know I don't like to be left alone, my darling.

Two shot—from angle which takes in the front door as she fusses around him, moving dishes, brushing his coat and babying him as she always does.

ALBERT: *(meekly)* I'm sorry, Mother.

MRS. LORY: *(looks at him accusingly)* And you had tobacco on your breath when you came home from that girl's house.

ALBERT: I only took a puff, Mother. I didn't like it.

MRS. LORY: I hope not! With your weak lungs tobacco could be the death of you. I'll always believe your dear father would have lived much longer if he hadn't smoked. It's poisonous to people who have sensitive nerves. Now me—

There is a knock at the door and she starts for it as she finishes her sentence.

MRS. LORY: *(continued)*—I can't stand the smell of tobacco in the house.

She opens the door and a German sergeant is seen in the doorway, two soldiers behind him. He is very polite. Speaks with a heavy accent.

MRS. LORY: *(continued) (bristles at them)* Now what do you want?

SERGEANT: *(looks straight past her at Albert who rises nervously)* Albert Lory?

Closeup—Albert. His face is absolutely paralyzed with fear and we see his face twitch. Then in a whisper, as if Sorel were invisibly at his ear, we hear Sorel's voice: "Dignity, Albert. Dignity." With an effort he controls himself and dignity seems to come into his expression.

Full shot in room, as the sergeant steps in followed by the two soldiers. Mrs. Lory herself is paralyzed for an instant. Then she springs in between them and her son.

MRS. LORY: What is it you want?

SERGEANT: Albert Lory. Hostage.

MRS. LORY: *(fiercely, blocking their way)* No! I won't let you do it! I won't let you take my boy! He's done nothing! He's innocent! Get out of my house!

SERGEANT: *(over above)* Bitte, bitte, gnadige frau! You don't make trouble now. We have orders. We do our duty.

While he is speaking the two soldiers step around them and take Albert's arms, swiftly searching him for weapons.

Close shot—soldiers searching Albert as we hear Mrs. Lory's frantic defiances. Albert stands frozenly, as if he didn't hear anything, hardly aware he is being searched.

MRS. LORY'S VOICE: Don't you touch him! Get out, get out! If you lay a hand on my son I'll go to our mayor. He knows my boy is innocent! Get out, I tell you!

The soldier who is searching Albert finds the illegal newspaper and calls to the sergeant as he pulls it out.

SOLDIER: Sergeant!

The sergeant enters frame with Mrs. Lory hanging on to his arm fiercely, but she is suddenly paralyzed as she sees the illegal newspaper which the soldier hands to the sergeant. Now the sergeant's manner changes toward Albert and he growls roughly.

SERGEANT: Where you get this?

ALBERT: *(blankly)* Under the door.

MRS. LORY: *(with a heart-rending cry)* Oh, Albert!

SERGEANT: *(brutal now, to soldiers, in German)* (Take him, take him!)

The soldiers now push Albert roughly between them toward the door as Mrs. Lory begins crying hysterically and follows, trying to pull her son away from them.

MRS. LORY: He's innocent, he's innocent! Let me tell you! He's innocent! Listen to me! Wait! I want to tell you!

But the ears of the soldiers are deaf as they take Albert out the door. The sergeant pushes the screaming woman back into the room and shuts the door in her face. She is crying hysterically and beating at the door as we

DISSOLVE OUT

DISSOLVE IN

INTERIOR SMALL ANTEROOM OUTSIDE VON KEL-
LER'S OFFICE—DAY
*Two German sentries stand at the heavy closed door that leads
into von Keller's headquarters. Half a dozen citizens are sitting
waiting in a row of chairs along wall outside door, their faces all
anxious, obviously relatives of hostages who have been taken:
Two middle-aged women, a young girl, a very old man with his
grandson beside him, and an old woman who is crying unashamedly. Mrs. Lory enters anteroom, walking with her cane
but not limping, her face grim and determined, just as Lieutenant
Schwartz comes out of the door between the sentries and motions
to the young girl. As the young girl enters nervously, Mrs. Lory
marches to the door and tries to enter but Schwartz closes the door
behind him and blocks her way.*
MRS. LORY: *(grimly)* Get out of my way, young man. I want to see
Major von Keller.
SCHWARTZ: I'm sorry, madam. He's very busy.
MRS. LORY: *(glares at him)* I'll wait till he's *not* busy.
SCHWARTZ: Have you an appointment?
MRS. LORY: You tell him it's Mrs. Emma Lory. I'm a very good
friend of the mayor's.
SCHWARTZ: I'm sorry, it's no use, madam. *(picks up from a small
desk an application form)* Write your name on this application and
the reason you want an interview. I'll let you know in a few days.
*With finality he goes into von Keller's office and leaves her
glaring at the closed door. She measures the sentries and they
move over in front of the door from either side. She flings down the
application form, turns and marches out aggressively, her cane
rapping on the polished floor.*

DISSOLVE OUT

DISSOLVE IN

INTERIOR SMALL ANTEROOM OUTSIDE MAYOR
MANVILLE'S OFFICE—DAY

74

Close shot. Mrs. Lory, very baffled now, confronts a self-important secretary who confronts her outside the mayor's door. Two policemen, even bigger and tougher looking than the German sentries we have just seen, stand guarding the mayor's door.

SECRETARY: *(impatiently)* I'm sorry, Mrs. Lory, he's having a meeting with the council. Impossible to see anybody.

MRS. LORY: *(indignantly)* If he won't see Emma Lory perhaps he'll see Emma Ballard. Forty years ago he got his face slapped for trying to kiss her.

SECRETARY: I'm sorry, I can't interrupt him. Come back tomorrow.

He goes into office as one of the policemen shuts the door behind him. Mrs. Lory looks angrily at the two policemen and finding no sympathy turns abruptly and marches out with her stick.

DISSOLVE

EXTERIOR DOOR OF GEORGE LAMBERT'S OFFICE—
DAY

Close shot—so we see the lettering "Superintendent, Freight Terminal."

Camera pulls back to take in Mrs. Lory who stands waiting and tapping her cane impatiently. The door opens and a little clerk wearing glasses and with a pencil behind his ear, black sleevelets on his arms to protect his shirt cuffs, steps out very importantly.

CLERK: Sorry, Mrs. Lory, the superintendent's very busy. He can't see you now.

This is the last straw for Emma and she raises her cane and flails at him. The little man ducks aside and the cane smacks the glass of the door and it shatters with a crash. She grasps the doorknob and marches straight in without a glance at the horrified little clerk.

INTERIOR GEORGE'S OFFICE—DAY

George has risen from his desk at the crash and looks at her with astonishment as she marches to his desk to confront him.

GEORGE: *(protesting)* Really, Mrs. Lory—

75

MRS. LORY: You listen to me, George Lambert! I'm not going to stand for any more nonsense! Do you know what they've done to my boy?

GEORGE: *(nods uncomfortably)* I'm awfully sorry.

MRS. LORY: Sorry, my eye! You're going to do something about it! Now you sit down and listen to *me*.

DISSOLVE

INTERIOR DINING ROOM OF MAYOR'S HOUSE—NIGHT
Medium shot—George Lambert facing the mayor across the dinner table. The table has not yet been cleared, the remains of the meal are there. The mayor has sent his wife and the servants out of the room. George has on a top coat and holds his hat, sitting facing the mayor, who is smoking a cigar. (Probably the mayor was in the living room, having coffee and his evening cigar, when George arrived unexpectedly.) Past them we can see into the entrance hall of the mayor's rather ostentatious home. In another wall is a door leading into living room. The door is closed but from the living room we hear the mayor's little girl practicing her scales on the piano with painful persistence—da da da da ta ti ta da da et cetera, over and over as the two men talk in foreground. On the dining room walls are a couple of large stuffed fish, proud catches of the mayor, and an oil painting of himself in the full regalia of his office. Furnishings in the usual bad taste. Now the mayor leans across the table, staring at George incredulously.

MAYOR: Paul Martin? . . . It's shocking! Incredible! *(gets up and stares up at his own portrait)* I've known Emma Lory for half a century. Her husband was my best friend—we both started in this town as young men, without a penny. She was a beautiful girl. She'd have done better if she'd married me. Lory had no spirit, no ambition—and he died before his son was born. *(turns to George, thinking of the past)* I even wanted to marry her then—but she was wrapped up in the boy. It's a fanatical devotion. We must remember, Lambert, she's the kind of woman who'd invent a story like this—accuse anybody—to save her son.

76

GEORGE: I wish I could believe that. But after she told me I did a little investigating. I found this concealed in the switch tower.

He brings out of his pocket a revolver and shows it. The mayor looks shocked.

MAYOR: That hangs him. The Germans don't joke about keeping firearms.

GEORGE: There's no proof yet that Paul hid it there . . . It could have been the relief man. *(righteously)* But if he's not guilty he can clear himself. I felt it was my duty to come here and put it up to you, sir.

MAYOR: Of course, Lambert.

The monotonous piano scales irritate him and he steps to the door, opens it and calls affectionately to the child we glimpse seated before the upright piano.

MAYOR: *(continued)* You'd better go to bed, Suzi. You've practiced enough.

As she slides off the chair eagerly—

MAYOR: *(continued)* Kiss papa first.

The little girl comes to the door and he kisses her and then shuts the door and comes back toward George who is watching him broodingly.

MAYOR: *(continued)* You've not only done your duty, Lambert— you can expect to be rewarded if Martin's the guilty man.

GEORGE: *(with revulsion, earnestly)* I want no reward, sir. It's very hard for me to do this.

MAYOR: *(sits down, facing him)* Between you and me, I hope he's the man. You know my problems—I have to handle von Keller with kid gloves. He told me today he has orders to increase shipments of meat and vegetables from this district. Our people are hungry enough as it is. It will certainly put von Keller in a good humor if I can deliver this saboteur. *(righteously, seeing the bitter expression in George's face)* Also, I save many lives. Not only Emma Lory's son, but my old friend Sorel.

GEORGE: Sorel's a radical. They won't let him go unless Paul tells who threw the bomb. *(suddenly angry at the injustice of it all)* The thing that makes me mad is the way he's fooled everybody. Me, his friend! Making friends with the Germans! I can't stand hypocrisy!

77

MAYOR: Neither can I. Everybody knows where I stand. They call me a collaborationist. Very well, I am. You know why.

GEORGE: *(nods broodingly)* It's easy for people in free countries to call us names. Wait and see what they do when the Germans march in. They'll shake hands and make the best of it.

MAYOR: *(dryly)* If they don't they'll get the worst of it. Between you and me, *(with virtuous finality)* I do my duty, Lambert. I'm mayor of the town and my duty is to defend it. Where can they find this fellow Martin? At home?

GEORGE: *(shakes head somberly)* He's on the night shift tonight. *(looks at his watch)* He should be at the switch tower in half an hour.

With the air of a man doing his highest duty the mayor gets up and goes to the telephone, George watching him broodingly.

MAYOR: *(into phone)* I want to speak to Major von Keller.

INTERIOR SMALL CAFE—NIGHT

Group shot. A gay group around a table, Paul Martin and three German soldiers, among them Karl and Otto. They are drinking beer and singing a sentimental German song which Paul is playing on the accordion. Or rather one soldier sings, knowing the words, and the other two try to follow. Paul makes a mistake and the singer laughingly corrects him, singing it correctly and beating time with his arms. Paul, grins, nods and picks up the air correctly. In background the proprietor leans on the zinc bar, watching them and listening. The windows and the glass of the front door are covered with blackout paper. We see the door opened a little and a girl peers in.

Close shot—Julie Grant as she opens the door a little wider, looking in past camera whence we hear the jolly singing and laughter. The eager expression fades from her eyes, and a look of disgust comes over her face, as she calls out over music:

JULIE: Paul!

Group shot. Paul looks around, sees her in the half-opened door and jumps up with a finishing flourish of the music. The Germans protest and half in German and half in English want him to continue.

OTTO: You don't stop, Paul.

78

PAUL: *(grins)* Don't be so friendly, Otto. You'll get me in bad with my girl.

OTTO AND KARL: *(calling to Julie in door)* Fraulein! Mademoiselle, you join us!

The girl ignores them and exits and Paul, thrusting the accordion into Karl's hands, waves good night to them laughingly as he runs to the door.

PAUL: Auf wiedersehen!

EXTERIOR DOOR OF CAFE—NIGHT

We see the bright light and Paul's figure against it as he exits. He stands blinking for an instant in the semi-darkness and then runs to catch up with Julie who has started walking fast.

EXTERIOR CAFE—SIDEWALK—NIGHT

Julie comes into camera as he catches up with her and stops her.

PAUL: Julie!

She is silent, frozen, and he peers at her anxiously.

PAUL: *(continued)* Why don't you answer me?

He takes her shoulders and pulls her around into close two shot so he can see her face, and we see tears glisten in her eyes.

PAUL: *(continued)* What is it?

JULIE: Nothing.

We hear a girl's laugh and both look past camera at:
Shooting past them along sidewalk we see a girl with a German soldier emerge from the gloom of the blackout the girl laughing. But as they come a couple of paces nearer the girl sees Julie and Paul and she averts her face from them, silenced, as she passes with the soldier. But after they have passed on out of scene we hear the girl laugh again, a different note, a forced bravado laugh, as if to tell Julie she's not ashamed. Julie and Paul have turned into camera, watching after the pair. Then Julie looks at Paul, tears flashing in her eyes as she breaks out in a low bitter voice:

JULIE: Why don't you go with a girl like that? Isn't she your type?

PAUL: Julie! *(draws her to him, his voice low and pleading)* I know what people say—but you've got to stick by me. Believe in me, Julie!

79

JULIE: *(pushes herself away from him)* I've tried to. But this is too much. I hate these soldiers. They killed my brother!
PAUL: Not these fellows, darling. He was killed at the front—before the armistice.
JULIE: *(looks at him and her eyes blaze)* I hate you too!
PAUL: *(trying to hold her as she backs off)* Julie!
JULIE: Don't touch me! Don't speak to me! I never want to see you again!

Her voice breaks and she runs off into the darkness.
Camera moves in close on his face as he stands looking after her, helpless to do anything, his eyes full of pain.

EXTERIOR RAILROAD YARD—NIGHT
Close shot of a man standing nervously at the edge of a box car on a siding. We hear trains moving out on the tracks out of scene. The man strikes a match and lights a cigarette and we recognize George Lambert. As he puts out match and we see only the glow of his cigarette, we hear the heavy tread of marching feet approaching. George looks past camera.
What he sees: Shooting past him we see a squad of a dozen German soldiers marching past silently in the semi-darkness.
Closeup—George as he looks in another direction at:
Medium long shot—another squad of soldiers marching silently toward the switch tower which looms in the distance across the maze of tracks.

EXTERIOR SWITCH TOWER—NIGHT
Full shot at base. We see German soldiers being deployed at various strategic points by an officer who only speaks in whispers. They move like shadows, all around.

EXTERIOR RAILROAD YARD—NIGHT
Medium shot—George Lambert waiting nervously behind end of box car. He hears what he has been waiting for, the footsteps of one man walking on cement and coming nearer. As they come very close George steps out, and camera pans to bring in Paul Martin who stops, surprised to find Lambert confronting him.

80

(There are enough train noises from out in the yard to cover their voices.)
PAUL: Hello, George.
George is silent, fumbling nervously for a cigarette. In background we see a train passing (Process).
Very close two shot as Paul looks at him wonderingly and George brings out a cigarette.
GEORGE: You're early. Have a smoke.
PAUL: *(feeling something is wrong)* Thanks.
Takes it and is about to strike a match, but George stops him.
GEORGE: Here's a light.
Paul is aware that George is watching him intently as he lights his cigarette from George's and hands it back.
PAUL: Thanks. Is anything wrong?
GEORGE: *(with repressed intensity)* You know I love Louise, don't you?
PAUL: Sure.
GEORGE: *(strangely)* You know what it means for me to lose her?
PAUL: *(relieved, thinking he understands George now)* Oh, she'll make up again.
GEORGE: *(bitterly)* I don't think so.
Paul peers at him wonderingly again, his manner is so strange.
GEORGE: *(continued)* Are you my friend?
PAUL: *(puzzled)* Why, sure.
GEORGE: Am I yours?
PAUL: Say, what *is* this?
GEORGE: *(very bitter)* You do something you know is right—and then you have doubts.
PAUL: What's the matter with you, George? What's worrying you?
GEORGE: *(sweat on his face)* Look. If you were in my place and you knew who did the sabotage, would you tell?
PAUL: *(suddenly realizes George is an informer)* Do you know who did it, George?
GEORGE: Yes.
PAUL: And you told?
GEORGE: Yes—*(bursts out in a low bitter voice as Paul looks at him strangely)* Why did you do it, Paul?

81

PAUL: Why did *you* do it, George?

GEORGE: *(bitterly)* Don't look at me like that!

PAUL: *(almost pitying him)* You're looking at yourself, George—
that's what you can't stand.

A train whistles out on the tracks, approaching.

PAUL: *(continued)* You can't stand it and that's why you're warning
me. Thanks, George.

*He is about to run out past camera toward the oncoming train
when we hear Julie's voice calling:*

JULIE: Paul! Paul!

*Paul turns as Julie comes running in from same way he himself
arrived. But he realizes every second counts.*

JULIE: *(continued) (breathlessly, almost crying)* Paul, I've got to talk
to you!

PAUL: *(swiftly)* Don't move, Julie—stay here!

*He pushes her into George's arms as he cries out above the
growing roar of the incoming train.*

PAUL: *(continued)* Hold her, George!

*And he springs out of scene past camera. Julie, not understanding
what it is all about, struggles to follow him, but George grips her
arms, watching after Paul with a stricken face.*

*What he sees—long shot across the tracks. A freight train is
coming through the railroad yard on the main track, rumbling
and rolling not very fast. We can see the dim figure of Paul
running for it, but it looks dubious if he can make it. As he sprints
diagonally, leaping across the glimmering streaks of the tracks, to
try to catch the caboose at the end, we hear shouts and shots as
German soldiers come running in from different directions.*

*End of train—moving shot—as Paul sprints in and just catches it
and climbs up. We hear shouts and shots from the darkness of the
yard as he climbs up swiftly.*

*Top of moving train. Shooting up toward the locomotive we see
Paul climb up on top in foreground and start running forward,
jumping from car to car. There is a volley of shots as he reaches
the third car and he collapses like a shot rabbit.*

*Top of box car—moving. Close downward shot on Paul Martin
sprawled out on his face, dead.*

82

FADE OUT

FADE IN

EXTERIOR FRENCH STREET—OUTSIDE PRISON
DOOR—DAY
*Wide angle on prison door, early next morning. An unknown old
woman, shawled and carrying a few pieces of firewood she has
collected, is passing along the sidewalk. Two German soldiers,
patrols, come striding past from opposite direction, but she
doesn't look at them.*
*Camera moves in close on door as we hear bolts clanking and the
small door (which opens from the big double doors of the prison
gate) is opened from within and Albert Lory steps out. The soldier
guard stands in the doorway behind him. Albert looks a little
dazed, like a man in a happy dream. He is unshaven, looks a trifle
dishevelled, his hair mussed, but otherwise perfectly normal. He
looks around a little confused and then turns politely to the soldier
guard who is in the act of closing the door.*
ALBERT: Good-bye. Thank you.
He walks happily past camera.

DISSOLVE

INTERIOR LORY HOME—DAY
*First a close shot at window and we see Louise's cat mewing
outside and rubbing against the glass. The window is opened by a
woman's hands and the cat comes in.*
*Camera pulls back swiftly to show that none other than Mrs. Lory
(a very different Mrs. Lory from the angry woman we last saw)
has let the cat in. Mrs. Lory bustles about, fixing the breakfast
table as usual. Then she hears a step and runs to the front window
and as she pulls back the curtain to look, the door opens and
Albert comes in, dishevelled as we saw him a few minutes ago.
Mrs. Lory puts her arms around him joyously and kisses him.*
MRS. LORY: Oh my boy! *My boy!*
ALBERT: *(all smiles)* Hello, Mother.

83

MRS. LORY: *(fussing over him joyously)* Oh, my poor boy! Just look at you! I didn't sleep a wink all night, thinking of you in that horrible filthy prison!

ALBERT: *(beams innocently)* But it was very nice, Mother. I saw Professor Sorel—he was in the cell right across from me. We talked all night—*(laughs)* and when the soldiers tried to listen, we talked in Latin.

MRS. LORY: *(smiling)* So you were having a good time while I was lying awake all night. That's just like a man—talk, talk, talk, and let the women worry.

ALBERT: *(puts his arm around her)* Oh, I worried about you, Mother. *(with a serious expression)* But Professor Sorel explained a lot of things to me I didn't understand. Now I know why our country fell—some people were more afraid of our own workers than they were of the enemy.

MRS. LORY: Nonsense!

ALBERT: No, look at our mayor. Maybe now he's very unhappy—it hasn't worked out the way he expected—but he was glad to shake hands with the German commander when they took over the town.

MRS. LORY: *(trying to silence him, spoofing at the very idea)* Sssh! You'll get into trouble talking like that. We must mind our own business.

ALBERT: *(a little puzzled)* But it *is* our own business, Mother. It's our land.

MRS. LORY: I don't need to be told that. I'm just living for the day when these Germans finish picking our bones and go.

ALBERT: But what's going to make them *go,* Mother?

MRS. LORY: I don't see why they don't have more privacy in that prison! Crowding people together! If you'd slept last night instead of talking to that old windbag you wouldn't look so tired.

ALBERT: *(not liking her talk)* I'm worried about Professor Sorel—they didn't release him. I'm the only one they let out. *(looks at her as if he'd just realized how peculiar that is)* Why *did* they let me out, Mother?

MRS. LORY: *(goes to table abruptly, very busy fixing his plate)* They aren't fools—they know you're needed at the school. Eat your breakfast, darling!

ALBERT: But Professor Sorel is needed more than I am.

MRS. LORY: Let's not ask questions. They'll let him out. Sit down. Eat your breakfast.

ALBERT: *(picks up the cat)* Before I eat I'm going to see Paul—and Louise.

MRS. LORY: *(whirls with frightened vehemence)* No, no, no!

ALBERT: But I must tell them I'm free. She'll be happy.

MRS. LORY: *(pale, as she looks at him)* No, Albert! No! Don't leave me!

ALBERT: *(peers at her anxiously)* What's the matter, Mother.?

MRS. LORY: I don't feel well—*(very pale)* and—and you must shave and change your clothes. You can't go out in the street the way you look.

ALBERT: But I just came through the street. It's only next door, Mother.

She is speechless, watching him with a tense pale face as he goes out with the cat in his arms. As the door closes behind him she sinks down into a chair.

EXTERIOR MARTIN HOUSE NEXT DOOR—DAY

Albert comes along sidewalk eagerly, carrying the cat, but suddenly stops short and stares at the door. Black crepe hangs on the front door. He looks shocked. Then he slowly goes to it and knocks fearfully and hesitantly.

Close shot—Albert at door, holding the cat. Again he knocks, panic coming into his face. He tries the doorknob and the door opens.

INTERIOR MARTIN HOUSE—DAY

Albert enters uneasily. He hears what we do—a sobbing anguished sound from the next room. He comes in close to camera and looks fearfully through:

Shot past his head into adjoining room. Julie Grant sits at a table, her head buried in her arms as she cries heart-brokenly. Louise is bent over her with one arm around Julie's shoulders, trying to comfort her.

Close shot—Albert as he stares past camera at the two girls.

85

ALBERT: *Louise!*
Close shot—Louise and the sobbing Julie. Louise straightens up and Julie lifts her tear-stained face, still crying brokenly. A look of fury and contempt comes into Louise's face.
Reverse angle—Albert, completely dazed, comes into the room towards them.
ALBERT: *(blankly)* Who—who—*(dazedly)* Where is Paul?
LOUISE: *(eyes blazing)* You coward! You know what happened to Paul! That's why you're free!
Albert, as if he had been struck in the face, makes a feeble gesture of denial with his arms and the cat falls to the floor. His lips move but he is too stunned to speak. Julie keeps crying.
LOUISE: *(continued) (blazing)* To think we trusted a thing like you! We knew you were weak but I told Paul you'd be strong enough to keep your mouth shut! *(contemptuously)* How much did they pay you? Or did they only give you your life? That's not worth much!
ALBERT: *(blubbering incoherently, his mind reeling)* Lo-Louise— *Louise—*
LOUISE: Don't try to lie! You're the only one who knew! Get out!
ALBERT: *(blubbering)* B-but, *Louise—*
LOUISE: *(fiercely) Get out!*
She strides over, pushes him out of the doorway and shuts the door in his face. Louise goes back and puts her arms around Julie and holds her close to her, as tender and full of compassion now as she was fierce a moment before.
LOUISE: *(continued)* Be proud, Julie! Let's be proud!
JULIE: *(brokenly)* Oh, I can't forgive myself for what I said to him.
LOUISE: *(drawing her close to her)* But he loved you for it! Don't you see?—he loved you for it!

EXTERIOR STREET IN FRONT OF MARTIN HOUSE—
DAY
Mrs. Lory is standing as grim as death, leaning on her stick, watching the crepe-hung door as it slowly opens and Albert emerges, sees nothing, his face blank, mouth slack, looking twenty years older. His legs seem to be caving under him as he starts to return home along the sidewalk and suddenly finds

86

himself confronting his mother. He blinks, looking at her as if he couldn't remember who she is. She takes hold of his arm, her voice hard.

MRS. LORY: Don't let that girl hurt you. She's mixed up in it too—just like that brother of hers. He was to blame for putting you in prison.

ALBERT: *(stammers blankly)* But he's—he's *dead.*

MRS. LORY: *(grimly)* And you're free, thank God!

He looks at her uncomprehendingly.

MRS. LORY: *(continued)* You might as well know now—I'm the one who told.

ALBERT: *(dazedly)* Told what, Mother?

MRS. LORY: *(her face hard with love for him)* I saw who climbed in the window the night you left me alone for this girl.

ALBERT: *(looks at her with a kind of horror growing in his eyes)* You—you told the Germans?

MRS. LORY: *(grimly)* I told George Lambert. He's your friend!

He stares at her wildly and then pushes her hand from his arm as he starts down the street and she cries out:

MRS. LORY: *(continued)* Albert!

EXTERIOR STREET—DAY

Shot on sidewalk as Albert comes walking like a man in a trance into camera, Mrs. Lory running after him. She catches his arm and stops him in close shot.

MRS. LORY: Albert! *Albert!*

ALBERT: *(jerks his arm free, rough with her for the first time in his life, and his voice is angry)* Go back! *Let me alone!*

She stands paralyzed, looking at him as he exits swiftly past camera, as if she can hardly believe it is her own son.

INTERIOR GEORGE LAMBERT'S OFFICE—DAY

Camera behind George who stands at the window near his desk staring out somberly at the maze of tracks where trains are switching and shunting and beyond them the switch tower rising stark against the gray ominous sky. A locomotive hoots in the distance and then we hear the chuff-chuff-chuff as it backs in on a siding. George seems to see nothing but the switch tower in the distance. From the next office we hear the swift clicking of typewriters, mingling in the symphony of sounds of the busy railroad terminal.

Closeup—George as he stares out window at the gray sky, absorbed in gloomy thought. He is looking at:

EXTERIOR SWITCH TOWER—DAY
Nearer shot, silhouetted against the cold sky.

INTERIOR GEORGE'S OFFICE—DAY
Close shot—George. A tormented look comes into his eyes. He starts out of his meditation, hearing the door open. As he turns, camera pans to take in doorway and von Keller comes in, very cheerful and pleasant.

VON KELLER: Good morning, Lambert. *(laughs exuberantly)* I feel poetic this morning. *(strikes a pose and declaims)* "Oh Romeo, Romeo—wherefore art thou, Romeo? Deny thy father and refuse thy name. Or, if thou wilt not, be but sworn my love, And I'll no longer be a Capulet." *(grins)* Shakespeare! Great man! We love him in Germany. The English don't understand him.

George looks at him somberly, tormented by his thoughts, and von Keller pulls up a chair expansively and sits down comfortably, indicating for George to sit down behind his desk.

VON KELLER: *(continued)* Sit down. You look as if you had indigestion. Or didn't you sleep well last night? Me, I slept better than I have for a week.

George has sat down gloomily and von Keller looks at him closely, a mocking glimmer in his keen eyes.

VON KELLER: *(continued)* Don't worry, my friend—she'll never know. We keep our secrets. Don't worry about that broken engagement—Now she'll be lonely and make up with you. *(watching George narrowly)* Too bad he wasn't taken alive. I think somebody warned him.

GEORGE: *(in a low voice, not looking at him)* Have you released all the hostages?

VON KELLER: By no means. Only that fool schoolmaster—*(grins)* After that scare I don't think we'll have any trouble keeping *him* in line. One for one—a fair trade and good business. *(softly)* I'm a good horse trader, Lambert: I don't open the net until I've caught all the fish. Unfortunately your friend Martin is dead, and dead men can't talk. *(leans forward, watching him closely)* But I've thought of a way to find his accomplices. Many people will be afraid to go to the funeral tomorrow. But you will go. You will comfort her. She will admire you for risking my displeasure—and when you take her home she'll want to cry on your shoulder. *(smiles)* You see, I make up your quarrel for you.

George just stares at him as if it were the devil speaking.

VON KELLER: *(continued)* She knows who the accomplices were— and you know the way to my office.

GEORGE: *(staring at him)* You think I'd do that?

VON KELLER: *(dryly)* I'm sure you will.

He gets to his feet cheerfully, George still staring at him, as the door opens and the little clerk (whom we saw Mrs. Lory strike at with her cane) comes hurrying in eagerly with something in his hands, then stops short at sight of von Keller.

CLERK: Oh, excuse me—I've got something for the superintendent.

VON KELLER: Come in, come in.

CLERK: *(to George, clutching a pigeon in his two hands)* We caught it in the trap, in the loft, sir. I thought maybe you'd like it for your dinner.

He brings it to George in his outstretched hands and von Keller smilingly strokes its neck as the little clerk, trying to curry favor with his boss, holds it out to George across the desk.

VON KELLER: Fine fat bird. I wouldn't mind having it on my own table.

George takes the bird into his own hands as von Keller exits.

VON KELLER: *(continued) (pointedly)* I'll expect to hear from you tomorrow night, Lambert. *(goes out)*

The little clerk stands waiting for some expression of thanks from George, but George is staring at the bird in his hands so strangely that finally the little clerk speaks nervously.

CLERK: I hope you like it, sir.

*He goes out. George sits stroking the bird and looking at it
strangely.*

EXTERIOR RAILROAD YARD—DAY
*Alongside tracks of terminal. Albert Lory is coming toward cam-
era which pans on him as he nearly bumps into von Keller who is
going opposite direction. Albert pays no attention and hurries on
as von Keller turns and looks after him, then goes on.*

INTERIOR GEORGE LAMBERT'S OFFICE—DAY
*Close shot—George at the dusty window. He opens the window a
little and lets the pigeon out. It flies away toward the switch tower
rising against the sky in the distance.*

EXTERIOR RAILROAD YARD—DAY
*Shooting up past the switch tower, black and gaunt against the
cold sky, we see the pigeon fly across it.*

INTERIOR GEORGE'S OFFICE—DAY
*George watches it until it is out of sight and then turns and goes to
his desk and opens a drawer, a strange look on his face.*

EXTERIOR DOOR OF GEORGE LAMBERT'S OFFICE—
DAY
*Shooting past the door we see Albert hurrying toward us with the
same distraught manner as when he left his mother. Just as he
reaches the door we hear a shot within the office. Albert flings
open the door and rushes in.*

INTERIOR GEORGE'S OFFICE—DAY
*Low camera beside desk shooting up at Albert as he rushes in and
stops short, staring down at a point just below camera. The rage
in Albert's face suddenly turns to shocked incredulity. For a
moment he stares rigidly, then comes forward and drops on his
knees. He touches something hesitantly which we cannot see
under camera.*
ALBERT: *(in a hoarse whisper)* George!

90

He lifts his hand and stares with a kind of horror at blood on his fingers. Mechanically fastidious, he takes his handkerchief and wipes the blood from his fingers. Then he reaches down, acting still with a kind of unthinking mechanical fascination, and picks up something—and we see a revolver. As he is holding it we see the door open in background and the little clerk peers in.
Close shot—little clerk peering in through door. His eyes widen and then leap with panic. Then he vanishes and we hear him running outside screaming:
CLERK'S VOICE: *Murder! Murder! Murder!*

FADE OUT

FADE IN

INTERIOR CHURCH—NIGHT
We see the little shrine of the prologue, but differently lighted now, for it is night. Votary candles burn before the small image of the Virgin. An old woman in a black shawl is knelt down before the shrine, but we cannot recognize her, seeing only her back, though her very posture shows intense suffering. A girl in black enters softly from behind camera, and we recognize it is Louise. She lights a candle, sets it before the image and starts to kneel down beside the praying old woman.
Reverse angle—Low camera close on the old woman as Louise kneels down into frame. The old woman lifts her head and we see it is Mrs. Lory. Louise looks at her, a little startled, and for a moment the two women look at each other. But grief has changed Mrs. Lory, the old antagonism with which she always looked at Louise is gone, and suddenly Louise, with tears in her eyes, puts her arm around Mrs. Lory's shoulder, and Mrs. Lory breaks, making a choking sound as we—

FADE OUT

FADE IN

EXTERIOR COURTHOUSE—DAY (RKO PATHE LOT)
Full shot of the old building with the statue in front of it (as is, except turn statue a little). In foreground on the side of a truck is a poster showing a German soldier holding a couple of poor children in his arms and the legend: "CITIZENS! TRUST THE GERMAN SOLDIER!" (See Life magazine for poster.) Beyond we see the empty plaza in front of the courthouse and about a dozen people straggling up the steps and into the door. A couple of German soldiers are watching, smoking cigarettes idly.

DISSOLVE

INTERIOR COURTROOM—DAY
A large simple room with white walls and plain benches. Three judges sit behind the bench at the far end. Below them is a table at which two clerks are taking down what the Prosecutor is saying to the jury at the left. At the right, Albert Lory sits mildly in the prisoner's dock between two policemen. It must be clear that this is a civil and not a military trial. The time is some days later and as we dissolve we are in the middle of the trial. The Prosecutor is confidently and unexcitedly summing up his case to the twelve townsmen in the jury box. He is a very dignified man, aware of his own importance, proud of his powers of speech and eager to please those in authority.

PROSECUTOR: Gentlemen of the jury, I wish to congratulate you on the fair way in which you have listened to the evidence in this case. We have always been proud of the way justice has been rendered in this court, and I am glad to say that the occupation hasn't affected it.
Reverse on spectators on the benches. Among them we see Mrs. Lory, strangely seated beside Louise, Julie next to Louise, Edmond Lorraine and his mother, a couple of citizens and then Lieutenant Schwartz at one side. The little pot-bellied man who "has indigestion" also sits in the front row.

PROSECUTOR'S VOICE: *(continues without break)* This is a civil trial and there has been no military interference.

92

Close shot—Albert between the two policemen in the dock. He listens quietly, but he looks stronger, there has been a growing of character in his face and even in the way he sits listening.

PROSECUTOR'S VOICE: *(continued)* I'm only sorry that the accused has refused to have a lawyer. I don't believe that the best lawyer in the country could contradict the evidence or shake our witnesses—

Close shot—lawyer and jurors listening. He smiles a little vainly as he adds:

PROSECUTOR: —but I have heard of cases where legal eloquence could soften the hearts of you gentlemen and save a guilty man's life if not his liberty.

Close shot—Mrs. Lory and Louise. Mrs. Lory stuffs a handkerchief against her mouth in her anguish and Louise tries to comfort her. (The tragedy has finally brought the two women together.)

PROSECUTOR'S VOICE: I must confess that I find it hard to demand the extreme punishment, as it's my duty to do, but I console myself with the fact that Albert Lory's own stubbornness is to blame.

Close shot—the three judges listening gravely.

PROSECUTOR'S VOICE: I can only sum up by saying that the murder has been proved—by the witnesses, by the gun which he was caught holding and which he admitted he held, by the blood on his handkerchief *and* by a very clear motive—

Close shot—Prosecutor taking in part of listening jury.

PROSECUTOR: —one of the oldest motives in criminal history— jealousy!

There is a very audible belch and the Prosecutor looks sharply around past camera at:

Close shot—several spectators in front bench, centering on the little pot-bellied man, who looks very innocent and deadpan.

Prosecutor and jury. The Prosecutor turns back to the jurors:

PROSECUTOR: You may find it preposterous to believe that a man of his years—

Close shot—Albert listening quietly in the dock.

PROSECUTOR'S VOICE: *(continuing without break)*—and timid character could become so enamoured of a young woman as to commit an act of violence to dispose of a vigorous and handsome rival.

Close shot—Prosecutor—taking in jurors as the Prosecutor smiles dryly for effect.

PROSECUTOR: Yet I've never seen any man too old to look at a charming young lady—and I wouldn't give my oath that such glances are always innocent.

Several jurors smile but there is an audible belch and the Prosecutor again looks sharply around past camera at:

Close shot—several spectators—centering on the little pot-bellied man, whose face is innocent of expression.

Prosecutor and jury. The Prosecutor turns back to the jurors righteously.

PROSECUTOR: Gentlemen, all I ask for is a just verdict.

Close shot—Mrs. Lory and Louise. Louise's eyes are indignant.

PROSECUTOR'S VOICE: The Prosecution rests.

Close shot—Albert in dock. His face is flushed, ashamed of the taunts of the Prosecutor. There is a buzz of spectators whispering in the room.

Close shot—judges. The presiding Judge in the middle looks at Albert past camera pityingly, his voice kind.

JUDGE: I must agree with the Prosecutor that this court regrets you have refused to be defended by counsel. You will have to address the jury from where you sit. You will be given all the time you wish, and I advise you to speak clearly and to the point.

Full shot as Albert gets to his feet and there is a hush in the room. The Prosecutor sits down very confidently and watches the accused ironically, as if to say "Watch this fellow make a fool of himself."

ALBERT: *(very politely and mildly)* Thank you, Your Honor. I will be very brief because I have written down all I have to say—

He reaches into his pocket for his paper but it isn't there. He begins to search his other pockets anxiously. Peers around behind him as if it might have dropped in the chair. Then searches his inner pockets again nervously as there are titters in the room.

ALBERT: *(continued)* I—I don't understand—I'm sure I had my papers—that's all I've been doing in my cell—writing it all down—

Close shot—Albert as, still searching feebly, he pulls his coat out and sees what we do—the torn lining of his inside breast pocket.

94

ALBERT: Oh—now I see—*(shows it innocently toward the judges)* It was just a little hole—but I've been away from home so long and—and nobody sewed it up.

Close shot—jurors, amused.
Close shot—Lieutenant Schwartz. No expression.
Close shot—Mrs. Lory and Louise. Mrs. Lory chokes a little watching her son.
Close shot—Albert as he turns to the jurors.

ALBERT: I—I hope you'll excuse me if I speak badly. I've never been able to speak in public. I know the Prosecutor has been making fun of me. I realize now that it's very easy to make fun of me—because I am ridiculous. I've always known I was ridiculous. And it's true I was jealous. That's ridiculous. I realize now I deserve to be laughed at—oh, not for loving a young girl, no one could help loving her, and it's a beautiful thing to love someone—but it was silly of me to have hopes, to dream that she would ever accept *me.*

Full shot as Albert touches his breast and he is so earnest that no one is smiling now.

ALBERT: *(with a little shame)* Being alone in my cell these days and nights, thinking, I've learned a lot of things. We forget what we look like. We imagine we're still young, even when we grow old. But this morning when I shaved I looked at myself, and I saw a very silly old man. But even that doesn't help things—you go on loving.

(There will be cuts to various people in the room during Albert's speech which are not indicated here.)

ALBERT: *(continued) (leans on the rail for a moment, thinking for a while)* But that's not what I'm on trial for. *(lifts his head and looks at jury earnestly)* I'm guilty of folly but not of murder. I hope the Prosecutor won't think I'm disrespectful to this court and the legal profession in not having a lawyer. My only defense is the truth. And no lawyer could know the truth as well as I do because I was there. I was the only one who was there. *(looks around appealingly)* I've always believed in the truth. Only sometimes you're blind and you can't see it. But then when somebody tells you, it's all clear, and you realize how stupid you were in believing lies. *(searching his own heart as they listen now in hushed silence)* The truth is I wanted to kill George Lambert. But I don't think I could have. *(looks at jury)* I'm

95

too weak. I'm a coward. Everyone knows it, even the Prosecutor— that's why he makes fun of me. *(touches his heart earnestly)* Oh, I'm not a coward in here. I have brave dreams, I'm not afraid to commit murder *here—(touches his head)*—but when I face reality outside I'm lost, I'm a coward. *(leans on rail thinking)* It's so strange. We're two people, all of us. One inside and one outside. *(then looks at jury again, struggling to speak his difficult thoughts)* George Lambert was two men. It wasn't till I saw him dead that I realized it—and I knew why he'd killed himself. He couldn't face reality. He was different from me: he was strong outside and weak inside. Inside *he* was a coward. And when this honest coward had to face what the other George, the brave George, had done, he couldn't stand it. So he killed himself. *(very puzzled)* It's strange, but I felt strong for the first time in my life when I saw him dead. And I was sorry for him. I suddenly understood everything. In a way I was responsible for his death—through my mother's love for me—

Albert turns and looks at his mother among the spectators; she is crying.

ALBERT: *(continued)* Even love can be a terrible thing—it can commit crimes.

Close shot—Albert as he looks at:

Close shot—Louise and Mrs. Lory. Mrs. Lory is crying while Louise listens as if she were seeing an Albert she has never known.

Close shot—Albert.

ALBERT: Louise, you thought I informed on Paul. It was my mother. To save me she told George. George told the Mayor who told Major von Keller, and Paul was killed.

Full shot as Albert turns to the jury quietly.

ALBERT: Even Mayor Manville is two men—but they're both strong. The outside man is saving the town while the inside man is saving himself.

Quick shots to startled reactions of jurors, judges, Schwartz and spectators. This sort of thing isn't in the book, it isn't expected. All lean forward uneasily as the Prosecutor jumps up and addresses the judges.

PROSECUTOR: I object, Your Honor. The accused has no right to seize this occasion to slander our Mayor who is an honorable man.

There is a very loud belch and the Prosecutor whirls around and points his finger at:
Close shot—little pot-bellied man, looking most innocent as the Prosecutor's voice rings out angrily:
PROSECUTOR'S VOICE: Your Honor, I demand that that man be ejected. He is deliberately mocking the dignity of this court of justice!

The little man rises politely and bows to the judges apologetically as he puts his hand on his fat stomach.
LITTLE MAN: *(meekly)* Excuse me, Your Honor—indigestion!

Close shot—Prosecutor glaring past camera at the little man.
Close shot—judges as the presiding judge nods gravely.
PRESIDING JUDGE: Proceed.
Full shot—courtroom as Albert turns to the judges innocently.
ALBERT: Excuse me, sir, if this is a court of justice I have a right to be heard. If I'm stopped now, how can anyone believe that our civil courts are dealing out justice under the Occupation, as the official newspapers insist?
PRESIDING JUDGE: *(red-faced)* Proceed.

Close shot—Schwartz. He looks very angry.
Full shot. Albert continues in a mild voice.
ALBERT: Thank you, sir. *(turns to jury, searching for words)* Even before the war our Mayor was convinced that our enemy was not the Germans but a part of our own people.
He stops as a guard comes hurrying in to the dock with some papers in his hand.
Close shot—Albert and the guard who extends the papers to him sotto voce.
GUARD: Here's your speech, Lory. We found it in the hall.
ALBERT: *(takes it)* Thank you—*(puts it in his pocket as if it were no longer useful or important)*

Close shot—Prosecutor. He looks very unhappy seeing Albert is going to continue extempore.
Full shot as Albert continues mildly.
ALBERT: Our Mayor was born poor, and then he became powerful—and he began to fear the very people he'd come from. Our country is full of men like that—every country is.

97

Close shot—Louise as, spellbound, with wonder in her eyes, she watches:

Close shot—Albert as he continues quietly.

ALBERT: George Lambert wasn't powerful—but he chose the side of the powerful men, he honestly admired them. And he found he got along better that way—

PROSECUTOR'S VOICE: *(sharply)* I object, Your Honor!

Full shot as Albert pauses. The Prosecutor has jumped up and continues:

PROSECUTOR: It's intolerable that the accused should exploit the freedom of this courtroom to indulge in dangerous political talk.

ALBERT: *(to the red-faced judges)* Maybe these things are political, sir—but they're the basis of my defense.

PROSECUTOR: *(angrily)* This is a court of justice, Your Honor!

A loud belch.

Close shot—Prosecutor as he turns and looks angrily past camera at:

Close shot—little pot-bellied man in the front bench as he puts his hand to his stomach and makes an apologetic gesture of innocent helplessness toward the Prosecutor.

Close shot—Prosecutor as he glowers and then turns back to the judges.

PROSECUTOR: Can the accused be permitted to slander the name of his unfortunate victim?

Full shot—courtroom. Albert turns to the judges patiently.

ALBERT: Is this a free court or not, sir?

PROSECUTOR: *(sharply)* If the accused insists on this kind of defense I request the court's permission to bring in a new witness.

PRESIDING JUDGE: Who?

PROSECUTOR: Mr. Henry Manville, Mayor of this town.

Albert peers at him.

PROSECUTOR: *(continued)* He's not present but I'll have him here in the morning. I request an adjournment.

PRESIDING JUDGE: *(to Albert)* Has the accused any objection?

ALBERT: *(politely)* Not at all, sir.

PRESIDING JUDGE: Very well. This session stands adjourned.

98

DISSOLVE

INTERIOR PRISON CELL—NIGHT
*Small stone-walled room, a cot, a chair, a table, a pail under the
bed. A heavy solid door opens on the corridor. In the opposite wall
a small barred window. Wooden shutters are closed outside the
bars. Albert sits on a stool in his shirt sleeves, his old coat on his
knees, deeply absorbed in trying to sew the torn pocket lining of
his coat. He does it very awkwardly. There is utter silence. After a
moment we hear an accordion outside, far away. Albert lifts his
head listening and we recognize the love song which Paul Martin
was playing the night Albert spied through the window of the
Martin house and saw Louise and the others. It brings Louise
before his mind's eye and he begins humming it softly and a little
off-key. He begins sewing again but stops abruptly as we hear the
bolt clank outside the heavy door. The door swings open and
Albert rises surprised as von Keller enters and nods to the jailer
who shuts and bolts the door behind him. Von Keller is very
amiable and polite.*
VON KELLER: Good evening, Lory—*(chuckles as he indicates the
coat in Albert's hands)* Ah, I heard about that torn pocket. You lost
your speech. But you did all right from all accounts—*(looks at the
bed)* May I sit down?
ALBERT: *(equally polite, peering at him innocently and curiously)*
Please. Of course.
VON KELLER: *(sits down and looks at him, very friendly)* Sit down,
Lory.
Albert sits down and von Keller studies him pleasantly.
VON KELLER: *(continued)* I was mistaken about you. You're a man
of real courage.
ALBERT: *(hardly believing his ears)* Oh, no—no—
VON KELLER: *(stops him with an upraised hand)* I know what you
said in court—but you're wrong. I know more about you than you do
yourself. *(smiles faintly)* I was a fool not to realize it sooner. *(takes out
his cigarette case, opens and extends it)* Cigarette?

Albert is just about to say no when to his own surprise he changes his mind. He takes one.

ALBERT: Thank you.

Von Keller lights it for him, watching his face, and he puffs awkwardly, holding it like a woman; then coughs and smiles apologetically through the smoke.

ALBERT: *(continued)* It's my second one.

VON KELLER: *(suddenly grins, and speaks sincerely)* Lory, I like you! *Von Keller lights his own cigarette and studies Albert, who shows no dislike of him.*

VON KELLER: *(continued)* It's too bad, you made a great mistake in court today. You called yourself a coward, but you disproved it by what you said. Now they know you killed Lambert.

ALBERT: *(very earnestly)* But I didn't.

VON KELLER: Now come, come, I'm not here to convict you, I want to save you. I'm your friend.

ALBERT: But I told the truth. I didn't.

Von Keller stares at him incredulously and it dawns on him that unquestionably the man is telling the truth.

VON KELLER: *(astounded)* Lory! I believe you! *(half to himself, with surprise)* And now I remember the way Lambert looked when I left him. *(staring at Albert)* It's incredible! *(very pleased with the situation suddenly)* That makes it very easy. Lambert was despondent because of losing Miss Martin—the police will find a suicide note. We can handle the jury and you'll be acquitted. *(beams at him)* You won't have to say another word in court.

ALBERT: *(watching him a little puzzled)* Did they find a suicide note?

VON KELLER: *(laughs)* You're a poet, Lory! A poet!

ALBERT: *(slowly)* I don't understand why you're trying to save me.

VON KELLER: I told you. I like you.

ALBERT: I see. You don't want me to say anything more in the courtroom.

VON KELLER: *(very friendly and confidential)* My dear Lory, it's a peculiar situation. A courtroom is a public forum. Of course we Germans could take over courts, schools, town halls, the administration of the whole country—but we're not tyrants—we prefer not to do that. We prefer to collaborate, to give freedom to the nations we

100

defeat on the battlefield. But freedom must be limited by the necessities of war. We're still fighting on other fronts. It's a very small sacrifice we ask of you, when we are still sacrificing our lives for the future happiness of the world.

Albert listens intently, his understanding expanding; von Keller smiles.

VON KELLER: *(continued)* You see I'm frank, I have nothing to conceal. I tell you these things because you're a man of intelligence. Lambert was just a tool, very honest but not very bright. The Mayor—you were right in the courtroom—he's working for his own interests. But—*(shrugs)*—we need them and we find them in every country we invade. *(smiles)* Even in Germany we used them. That was the way our Party got into power. They're everywhere. *(with a touch of fanatical faith)* That's why nothing can stop us from winning the world. America feels secure because of her oceans—they think of invasion in terms of armies and airplanes—but they're *already* invaded. The honest Lamberts and the dishonest Manvilles are waiting to welcome us—just as they did here in Europe. *(smiles ironically)* And if at any time we need peace—if peace becomes a further weapon of conquest—their sincere patriotism will find plenty of arguments for the peace. *(laughs)* After all, what is the United States? A charming cocktail of Irish and Jews. Very spectacular but childish. And England? A few old ladies wearing their grandfathers' leather britches. *(gets up, very pleased with himself)* Well, what do you say, Lory?

ALBERT: *(rises politely)* Thank you—could I have another cigarette?

VON KELLER: *(laughs as he takes out his case)* All you want, all you want!

ALBERT: *(taking one)* Thank you. Just one.

Von Keller raps on the door for the jailer, then looks at Albert who watches him curiously.

VON KELLER: Lory, I'm glad you've decided to live—and be a free man. You're a schoolmaster and you have a great duty—the regeneration of the youth. You have to make them ready for the world of tomorrow—and believe me, it will be a fine world.

The jailer opens the heavy door from the outside and he goes out. Albert slowly sits down, thinking, thinking, and the accordion music continues sweetly in the distance, though now he is oblivious of it.

FADE OUT

FADE IN

INTERIOR ALBERT'S PRISON CELL—DAY
It is early morning and the shutters have been opened so we see the bars against the bright sky. Albert has his shirt off and looks a little absurd, plumply absurd, as he shaves himself, peering at a little metal mirror which is propped on a ledge of the stone wall. His face is lathered. As we have faded in we have heard the feet of tramping soldiers somewhere outside and now they grow louder, ringing on stone flagging as they pass. Albert stops shaving to listen. He tries to see out through the small barred window but it is too high. He gets the stool and climbs up on it shakily.

EXTERIOR SMALL BARRED WINDOW—DAY
Albert's lathered face appears behind bars. He sees:

EXTERIOR COURTYARD—DAY
Reverse angle—long shot—ten civilians lined up against a wall and a firing squad deployed in front of them.

EXTERIOR WINDOW OF PRISON CELL—DAY
Closeup—Albert as seen through bars. A wild look comes into his eyes.

EXTERIOR COURTYARD—A WALL—DAY
Near shot on the ten civilians. Closest to camera is Sorel, next Mr. Lorraine, next the three printers we saw arrested, and five other citizens. Suddenly we hear Albert's voice screaming from a distance:
ALBERT'S VOICE: Professor Sorel! *Professor Sorel!*
Sorel looks off, but sees foggily, having on the wrong glasses. Automatically he reaches into his handkerchief pocket, gets out

his far-seeing glasses, puts them on, recognizes Albert—smiles and waves.

EXTERIOR BARRED WINDOW OF ALBERT'S CELL—DAY
Close into Albert's face as seen through bars as he screams:
ALBERT: *PROFESSOR SOREL!*
There is an explosion—a volley of rifles—and he flinches and closes his eyes as he whispers:
ALBERT: *(continued)* Professor Sorel!
Then he opens his eyes and looks, the frenzy going from his face which seems to fill with strength and resolution. It is as if the explosions of their rifles had smashed through a window in his mind and now he sees a new and unknown world.

DISSOLVE

EXTERIOR COURTHOUSE—DAY—(RKO PATHE)
Full shot—courthouse. A dozen German soldiers are here in the plaza today, keeping an eye on a crowd of townspeople flocking up the steps and into the courthouse. The little pot-bellied man comes hurriedly in from behind camera, briskly heading for the steps.

EXTERIOR COURTHOUSE DOOR—DAY
Medium shot taking in the doorway through which people are flocking. In foreground a German soldier is keeping a cold eye on those entering. The little pot-bellied man comes hurrying up steps and starts to go in but the soldier reaches out and blocks his way with a stern arm. The little man looks at the soldier with innocent pleading but the soldier shakes his head and gestures with his thumb for him to get the hell out of there. The little man belches loudly in the face of the soldier, indicates his stomach apologetically and turns away, exiting from scene.

DISSOLVE

INTERIOR COURTROOM—DAY

Full shot. Albert is already in the prisoner's dock between the two guards. Jurors and judges seated, as are all the spectators. The room is crowded now. On the front bench is a new figure, Mayor Manville, waiting to be called. Louise sits with Mrs. Lory and Julie. Schwartz sits off inconspicuously at one side with his notebook.

PRESIDING JUDGE: You may call your witness, Mr. Prosecutor.

PROSECUTOR: *(rises with the important pleased manner of a man who is going to right a great wrong)* If the court pleases, it will not be necessary to call Mayor Manville. Happily for the cause of justice new evidence has been found which will make unnecessary the continuation of this trial.

Close shot three judges as they lean forward and we see they are not a party to this business. All very curious.

PRESIDING JUDGE: What evidence? Why hasn't the court been informed of this?

Full shot as prosecutor goes to bench with a piece of paper in hand.

PROSECUTOR: I only found it this morning, Your Honor, among some mail which I'd forgotten to open. It's in the handwriting of the deceased George Lambert and was mailed at the railroad station shortly before his death.

He hands it up to the judge and the two other judges lean close to look at it.

PROSECUTOR: *(continued)* I offered it in evidence.

Close shot Albert who leans forward, confounded.

PROSECUTOR'S VOICE: It saves us from a serious miscarriage of justice because it clearly shows that the deceased George Lambert intended suicide.

Close shot—Mrs. Lory and Louise. Louise listens with an intent face but Mrs. Lory's face floods with joy. Albert's voice rings out:

ALBERT: Excuse me, Your Honor—it's a forgery!

Full shot. Everyone is rigid as the prosecutor whirls on Albert who stands in the dock, leaning on the rail. The words are a bombshell.

ALBERT: I know all about that letter—but I didn't know it was going to be mailed to the prosecutor—I mean I didn't know he was going to write it—I mean—

PROSECUTOR: Quiet, you fool!
PRESIDING JUDGE: *(raps)* Just a moment, Mr. Prosecutor. *(looks at Albert)* What *do* you mean, Lory?
ALBERT: The letter's forged. Major von Keller told me last night.
PROSECUTOR: *(savagely)* He's out of his mind! The man's insane.!

INTERIOR COURTROOM—DAY
Close shot—Mrs. Lory and Louise in front seat. Mrs. Lory, frantic, starts to get up but Louise pulls her down beside her firmly, leaning forward and watching Albert intently.
Full shot—courtroom as Albert calls out vigorously to the judges.
ALBERT: No, Your Honor—I'm not insane! The prosecutor wrote that letter to himself . . . He's trying to save my life!
There is a sharp laugh and then the whole room goes into a roar of laughter at the apparent hilarity of the situation, and the comedy is heightened by Albert's earnestness. The judge pounds in vain for order to be restored and finally the laughter dies away as the prosecutor strides over before the judges indignantly.
PROSECUTOR: *(angrily)* This is certainly no laughing matter, Your Honor. For the sake of the dignity of this court I respectfully ask that the man who started that unseemly outburst be forcibly removed from this room!
Close shot—judges.
PRESIDING JUDGE: The court agrees with you, Mr. Prosecutor. *(looks past camera sternly at spectators)* Which of you started that laughter? Please stand up.
Reverse on spectators. Nobody moves. They are almost grim and defiant now.
JUDGE'S VOICE: I ask you again. Who started that laughter?
Nobody moves.
Close shot—Albert as he turns to the judges in the utter silence.
ALBERT: *(quietly)* I can guess who it was, Your Honor: The Unknown Soldier.
Full shot on faces of spectators. The defiance goes from their faces, they are deeply moved.
Close shot—prosecutor standing in front of judges and taking in the presiding judge. The prosecutor bites his lip, completely

floored. The judge is looking past camera at Albert with some amazement and his voice is more full of respect than it has ever been before.

PRESIDING JUDGE: Proceed, Mr. Lory.

Close shot—Albert.

ALBERT: *(very earnest)* Thank you, sir. I found out last night that I'm a very lucky man—that this is the only place left in my country where a man can still speak out—standing where I stand now.

Full shot. The prosecutor interrupts.

PROSECUTOR: Excuse me, Your Honor, I ask that the courtroom be cleared.

ALBERT: He's afraid, Your Honor. He's trying to deprive me of my last chance to speak. I know I'm a condemned man. I know I will die. Are you going to let me speak, Your Honor, or are you afraid, too?

PROSECUTOR: I demand that the courtroom be cleared.

PRESIDING JUDGE: Proceed, Mr. Lory.

Close shot—Albert as tears come into his eyes. He knows the danger the judge is risking.

ALBERT: Thank you. Thank you, sir.

Close shot—Louise and Mrs. Lory. Joy in Louise's face and absolute despair in Mrs. Lory's.

Close shot—Mayor Manville. He looks very angry and uneasy, as if he'd like to be out of the room.

Full shot as Albert turns to the jury but addressing the whole crowded room.

ALBERT: I'm a very lucky man. I had a moment of weakness last night—I wanted to live. And I had good reasons to live. Major von Keller told me beautiful things about the future of this world they're building. I almost believed him. It's very hard for people like you and me to understand what is evil and what is good. It's easy for working people to know who the enemy is because the aim of this War and this Occupation is to make them slaves. But middleclass people like us can easily believe as George Lambert did—that a German victory isn't such a bad thing. You hear people say that too much liberty brings chaos and disorder. That's why I was tempted last night by Major von Keller when he came to my cell. *(now in wonderful control not only of himself but of the whole crowded room)* But this morning I

106

looked out through bars and saw this beautiful new world working. I saw ten men die because they still believed in freedom—*(with emotion)*—and among them was a man I loved, Professor Sorel. He smiled and waved to me, as if he were telling me what to do. I knew then I had to die—and the strange thing is I was happy.

PROSECUTOR: *(white-faced and grim)* Your Honor, I demand an adjournment. I object to this insane talk!

PRESIDING JUDGE: Quiet, please.

ALBERT: *(looks at the judges, very proud and happy)* Those ten men died because of Paul Martin. But they didn't blame Paul Martin—they were proud of him. Paul was a soldier. Without glory but in a wonderful cause. I see now that sabotage is the only weapon left to a defeated people—and so long as we have saboteurs the other free nations who are still fighting on the battlefields will know that we're not defeated. I know that for every German killed, many of our innocent citizens are executed. But the example of their heroism is contagious, and our resistance grows. It's very easy to talk about heroism in the free countries—but it's hard to talk about it here where our people are starving. The hard truth is that the hungrier we get the more we need our heroes. We must stop saying that sabotage is wrong, that it doesn't pay . . . It does pay. It makes us suffer, starve and die—but though it increases our misery it will shorten our slavery. That's a hard choice, I know. *(eyes glow with his belief)* But even now they are bringing more troops into this town because of the trouble that has started—and the more German soldiers here the less they have on the fighting fronts. Even an occupied town like this can be a fighting front too—and the fighting is harder. *(looks around the room with compassion)* We not only have to fight hunger and a tyrant. First we have to fight ourselves. This Occupation—any Occupation in any land—is only possible because we are corrupt. *(touches his heart)* I accuse myself first. The flesh is weak. For my own comfort and security I made no protest against the mutilation of truth in our schoolbooks. My mother got me extra food—and milk—by a subterfuge, and I accepted it without facing the fact that I was depriving children and people poorer than we were of their portion. *(points at a juror)*

    Close shot—Mr. Noble in the jury box.

ALBERT'S VOICE: You are the butcher, Mr. Noble. Naturally you wanted to survive—and the black market was the answer. You keep your business going by selling meat out the back door at ten times its price. Some to my mother, who was equally guilty, as I was in eating it.

Close shot—Mr. Milette next to Noble. He begins to wither at the sound of Albert's voice.

ALBERT'S VOICE: You, Mr. Milette, are doing very well in your hotel, even though it's filled with Germans. You've never sold so much champagne and at such a good price. Of course, they print the money for nothing but with this money you're buying properties, just as the mayor is.

INTERIOR COURTROOM—DAY
Close shot—all jurors.

ALBERT'S VOICE: I could say the same about many of you. If the Occupation lasts long enough the men who are taking advantage of it will own the town. I don't blame you for making money—you should blame yourselves for making the Occupation possible—because you can't do these things without playing into the hands of the real rulers of the town, the Germans.

INTERIOR COURTROOM—DAY
Full shot. Everyone is spellbound as Albert looks at the juror.

ALBERT: That's why I know you must condemn me to die. Not because I killed George Lambert, which I didn't, but because I've tried to tell the Truth. And the Truth can't be allowed to live under the Occupation. It's too dangerous. This Occupation lives upon lies, just as the whole evil world they call the New Order does. Officially you will find me guilty of murder—

Close shot—Albert as he leans toward them, helpful and compassionate.

ALBERT: But don't worry, my friends. Even if you acquitted me and I walked out of this courtroom a free man, the enemy would take me and put me against a wall.

Close shot—jurors spellbound.

108

ALBERT: And you, too. They can find any reason to take hostages. *(then he turns and looks at Louise, smiling a little)* There's one final charge I must answer to, and I'm very guilty. Yesterday I was ashamed when the Prosecutor accused me of loving you, Louise.

Close shot—Louise, as she listens, her face glowing with pride and love for him.

ALBERT'S VOICE: *(triumphantly)* It's true. I've always loved you, secretly. But now I'm not ashamed. I'm proud, and I don't want to keep it a secret. I want to tell the whole world.

Tears in Louise's eyes.

Close shot—Albert, as he smiles at her tenderly and proudly.

ALBERT: I don't feel silly at all. Maybe it's because I'm going to die— but I feel very young. *(leans on the rail and looks around the room, shyly proud, as if confiding another secret)* Last night Major von Keller told me something very funny. He told me I wasn't a coward— *(laughs)* I think he was right.

He turns and looks at:

Close shot of the three judges listening with smiling dignity.

ALBERT'S VOICE: And I think I'm not the only one who's not a coward—

Full shot—as he looks all around the room proudly.

ALBERT: This town is full of courage. I'm proud of it. I'm proud to be born and die here. *(turns to judges again)* Thank you, Your Honors.

The whole crowded room sits spellbound, in hushed silence, as he sits down. Here and there we hear and see people crying.

Close shot—Louise and Mrs. Lory. Mrs. Lory is weeping hopelessly and silently while Louise watches Albert with a transfigured face, tears of joy in her eyes, loving him as she has never loved any human being. We hear the judge's gavel.

Full shot. The presiding judge addresses the jurors.

PRESIDING JUDGE: Gentlemen of the jury, you will now retire from this courtroom to exercise your free conscience and arrive at a just verdict.

To everyone's astonishment, including Albert's, the president of the jury, Mr. Noble, the butcher, stands up in the box.

MR. NOBLE: We've already agreed on the verdict, Your Honor.

PRESIDING JUDGE: Albert Lory. Please stand.

109

Albert rises, a little bewildered, peering at the jurors, whom the judge addresses.

PRESIDING JUDGE: *(continued)* What is the verdict?

MR. NOBLE: *(facing Albert)* We, the jury, by unanimous agreement and fully conscious of our responsibility in weighing the guilt or innocence of the accused, who has here been tried for the murder of George Lambert, find him not guilty.

Close flash—Albert absolutely stunned.

Full shot as Albert stands speechlessly, the spectators throw all caution to the winds, getting to their feet, some of them cheering, some breaking past the attendants to run to the jury box and grasp the hands of the jurors, some crying with joy and excitement. The judge is pounding his gavel for order as Louise struggles through the crowd to get to Albert and we—

DISSOLVE

EXTERIOR STREET—DAY

Camera moves along on the two happiest people in the world— Albert and Louise. They come walking along the sidewalk like two children, unashamedly holding hands, and Louise's face is transfigured, bursting with pride of Albert, who is equally proud of her—his face glowing with joy and pride and dignity. We hear the accordion gaily playing the love song which is like a theme of their love. But the most stupendous thing of this walk which is a triumphal march through the town, is the reaction of the citizens they pass and who come flocking out of the doorways and leaning out windows to get a glimpse of their great man. They stand aside with respect, lifting their hats almost solemnly and Albert gaily nods and smiles this way and that to them as he passes. Suddenly the little pot-bellied man, who is afflicted with "indigestion" comes hurrying out of a doorway, steps in close as he takes off his hat respectfully, seizes Albert's hand and shakes it, tears in his eyes. Then he steps back, holding his hat, as Albert passes on with Louise. As more and more citizens come flocking out to pay their proud tribute to him, we begin to hear schoolbells ringing over the

110

*music, the bells growing louder as they near the school—and even
the bells are gay and happy.*

DISSOLVE

INTERIOR ALBERT'S CLASSROOM—DAY
*All the rowdy boys are in their seats, the full class including little
Edmond Lorraine, a black band on his sleeve, and the bells are
still ringing though more softly now. For a moment perhaps we
think the boys are going to be up to their old pranks and be the
only ones in town to show disrespect, but as the bell dies away, the
door opens heartily, not hesitantly and fearfully as Albert used to
open it, and Albert comes striding in, really looking young—and
incredibly happy. Louise stops in the doorway, for a moment
fearing the boys are going to misbehave, but as Albert smiles at his
class the two rowdies, Julian and Henry, stand up abruptly and
the other boys look at them and all spring to their feet, standing
straight and stiff, showing even more respect for their schoolmaster than the townspeople did.
Full shot. Albert goes to his desk and leans on it for a moment,
beaming at the hushed attentive boys. His manner now is almost
as Sorel's was.*
ALBERT: *(cheerfully)* Thank you, young men. Sit down.
*He takes a book from his pocket as Louise comes over behind him
watching proudly.*
ALBERT: *(continued)* I'm afraid this is my last class. I don't know
how much time I have—but if it must be a short lesson, I think I've
found the best book. *(looks at the worn book in his hand)* Professor
Sorel gave it to me—*(drops his voice and confides to them smilingly)*—and the only reason it wasn't burned with the others is
because I hid it away in my bedroom. *(opens the book; cheerful, but
very serious now)* I'm going to read you something that was written by
great men, written in a night of enthusiasm a long time ago. A
hundred and fifty years ago. These men came from all classes—
aristocrats, working people, businessmen, men of religion—and they
didn't fight with each other, they all agreed on that wonderful night.
(looks at book) Now other men are trying to destroy this book. Maybe

111

this copy will be burned. But they can't burn it out of your memories. You'll have to rewrite it some day. *(looks at them proudly)* That's why you young people are so important. You're going to be the new nation. *(looks at book and reads and you could hear a pin drop)* "A Declaration of the Rights of Man: *(reads and his voice grows clear and strong)* Article One: Men are born and remain free and equal in rights. Article Two: The purpose of all political parties is the safeguarding of the natural and inalienable rights of man. These rights are liberty, property, security, and resistance to tyranny."

Boys' faces listening raptly as he continues.

ALBERT'S VOICE: "Article Three: The principle of all government resides in the nation itself. No group, no individual, can exercise any authority which does not expressly emanate from the people."

Full shot—as Albert continues, Louise near him watching. A wonderful silence and attention.

ALBERT: "Article Four: Liberty consists in freedom to do all that does not harm others. Article Five: The law has the right to forbid—"

He breaks off reading as the door is flung open and two German soldiers enter followed by the tough sergeant we have seen before. Louise flinches and pales but Albert is unfrightened, addressing the soldiers who motion for him to come with them.

ALBERT: *(continued)* Just one moment, gentlemen. *(turns to class and finishes reading)* "Article Five: The law has the right to forbid only those actions which are harmful to society." *(closes the book quietly and looks fondly at the wide-eyed children)* I'm sorry, I must go. I must go not because I'm harmful to society, which is you, but harmful to tyranny—

And he indicates the soldiers without malice.

SERGEANT: *(curtly)* That's enough. Come on!

Albert closes his book and puts it on the desk before him. He looks at Louise and suddenly she puts her arms around him and kisses him with her whole heart and soul, crying as she clings to him. Gently he releases himself.

ALBERT: Don't move. Don't move, Louise. Don't cry. I'm happy. *(turns to children)* Good-bye, citizens.

With a firm step he walks out between the two soldiers without a backward glance. The sergeant shuts the door and Louise is left alone with the children. She is still crying. Then she hears a boy crying and sees it is the toughest boy in the class, Julian Lamont. Louise shakes her tears away, steps to the desk, opens the book and begins reading in a firm voice:

LOUISE: "Article Six: The law is the expression of the will of the people. All citizens have the right to assist personally, or through their elected representatives, in its formation. It ought to be the same for all, whether it protects or whether it punishes. All citizens, being equal in the eyes of the law, have equal rights to all dignities, places and public positions according to their capacity, and without other distinctions than those of their virtues and talents."

As she is reading, we quietly—

FADE OUT

THE END